Working with Bilingual Children

BILINGUAL EDUCATION AND BILINGUALISM

Series Editor
Professor Colin Baker, *University of Wales, Bangor.*

Other Books in the Series
Building Bridges: Multilingual Resources for Children
 MULTILINGUAL RESOURCES FOR CHILDREN PROJECT
A Parents' and Teachers' Guide to Bilingualism
 COLIN BAKER
Policy and Practice in Bilingual Education
 O. GARCIA and C. BAKER (eds)
Teaching Science to Language Minority Students
 JUDITH W. ROSENTHAL

Other Books of Interest
Asian Teachers in British Schools
 PAUL A. S. GHUMAN
Citizens of This Country: The Asian British
 MARY STOPES-ROE and RAYMOND COCHRANE
Continuing to Think: The British Asian Girl
 BARRIE WADE and PAMELA SOUTER
Coping with Two Cultures
 PAUL A. S. GHUMAN
Education of Chinese Children in Britain and the USA
 LORNITA YUEN-FAN WONG
Equality Matters
 H. CLAIRE, J. MAYBIN and J. SWANN (eds)
European Models of Bilingual Education
 HUGO BAETENS BEARDSMORE (ed.)
Foundations of Bilingual Education and Bilingualism
 COLIN BAKER
Language, Minority Education and Gender
 DAVID CORSON
Making Multicultural Education Work
 STEPHEN MAY
Three Generations - Two Languages - One Family
 LI WEI
The World in a Classroom
 V. EDWARDS and A. REDFERN

Please contact us for the latest book information:
Multilingual Matters Ltd,
Frankfurt Lodge, Clevedon Hall, Victoria Road,
Clevedon, Avon BS21 7SJ, England

BILINGUAL EDUCATION AND BILINGUALISM 6
Series Editor: Colin Baker

Working with Bilingual Children

Good Practice in the Primary Classroom

Edited by
Mahendra K. Verma,
Karen P. Corrigan and Sally Firth

MULTILINGUAL MATTERS LTD
Clevedon • Philadelphia • Adelaide

Library of Congress Cataloging in Publication Data

Working With Bilingual Children: Good Practice in the Primary Classroom/
Edited by Mahendra K. Verma, Karen P. Corrigan and Sally Firth
(Bilingual Education and Bilingualism: 6)
Includes bibliographical references and index
1. Language and languages–Study and teaching (Primary)–Bilingual method.
2. Children of minorities–Education (Primary)–Great Britain. 3. Bilingualism in children–Great Britain. 4. Education–Great Britain. 5. Education, Bilingual–Great Britain. 6. English language–Study and teaching (Primary)–Foreign speakers. 7. English language–Study and teaching (Primary)–Great Britain.
I. Verma, Mahendra K., 1937- . II. Corrigan, Karen P., 1961- . III. Firth, Sally, 1968- . IV. Series.
P53.25.W67   1995
371.97′00941–dc20   95-6555

British Library Cataloguing in Publication Data

A CIP catalogue record for this book is available from the British Library.

ISBN 1-85359-294-3 (hbk)
ISBN 1-85359-293-5 (pbk)

Multilingual Matters Ltd

UK: Frankfurt Lodge, Clevedon Hall, Victoria Road, Clevedon, Avon BS21 7SJ.
USA: 1900 Frost Road, Suite 101, Bristol, PA 19007, USA.
Australia: P.O. Box 6025, 83 Gilles Street, Adelaide, SA 5000, Australia.

Typeset by Action Typesetting, Gloucester.

Contents

Introduction

MAHENDRA K. VERMA, KAREN P. CORRIGAN AND SALLY FIRTH

The teaching of English as a Second Language to minority school children and to their refugee or immigrant parents has led to much educational and political debate among teachers, parents, educationalists and politicians alike. Plowden (DES,1967), Bullock (DES,1975), Rampton (DES,1981), Swann (DES,1985) and, more recently, the National Curriculum documents, have discussed the English language development of these bilingual or potentially bilingual children to greater or lesser extents. A fundamental feature of these debates has been the concern of teachers and instructors regarding four major aspects of their work with bilingual children:

(1) the lack of opportunity on teacher training courses to equip educators sociolinguistically and pedagogically to meet the cultural and linguistic needs of the bilingual child;
(2) job insecurity given the unstable nature of Section 11 funding, and the consequences on ESL planning;
(3) the lack of parity in status between bilingual support and mainstream teachers; and
(4) the frustration engendered by continual exposure to racism and prejudice both within schools and society.

The 'Working with Bilingual Children' project based in the Department of Language and Linguistic Science at the University of York, was an attempt to extend the pre-National Curriculum research reported by Bourne (1989) into the post-National Curriculum period, and to inquire into the expansion of ESL provision at the cost of bilingual support. As the project was committed to working in close partnership with the staff supporting bilingual children, it was decided to organise two In-Service Training courses for teachers working within the primary classroom.

The first 'Working with Bilingual Children' INSET was held at the

University of York in March 1992 and the second was held there in April 1993. They arose as a direct response to the findings of research between September 1991 and September 1994 by Verma, Corrigan and Firth into bilingualism in UK primary schools, funded by a University Funding Council Continuing Education Grant for a Short Course Development Project and by an additional award from Humberside LEA. The courses were attended by both mainstream and support teachers working with bilingual children in primary schools throughout Britain. They considered how to help bilingual children's cognitive and linguistic potential and improve language awareness amongst teachers, by covering areas such as:

- Bilingual language learning theories;
- Bilingual children's classroom language;
- Supporting new arrivals as they acquire English;
- Bilingual children and the National Curriculum;
- The relationship between the support teacher and the classroom teacher;
- Assessment of bilingual children;
- Language development of bilingual children at home and in school;
- Classroom-based research on spoken and written discourse;
- Recent research in bilingual education;
- Strategies for supporting bilingual children in the classroom.

Three of the major Governmental reports on language, education and curriculum, namely, Bullock (DES,1975), Kingman (DES,1988) and Cox (DES,1989) emphasise that the future of 'knowledge about' or 'awareness of language' as a viable component of any curriculum depends upon adequate teacher training. However, in a survey conducted by Brumfitt (1988) on behalf of the National Congress on Language in Education (NCLE), it was revealed that only nine out of 33 Universities and seven out of 26 polytechnics had made language awareness a compulsory module in the pre-service education of teachers. Given this differential between policy and practice, the DES provided funding between 1989 and 1992 for the so-called LINC project, the aim of which was to produce teacher-training packages to assist with the teaching of language awareness in the National Curriculum. Unfortunately, permission was rescinded for the official publication of these materials in 1991 on the authority of the Minister for Education. Thus, despite the fact that some of these have since been published independently by members of the research team (notably, Carter 1992), their contribution to actual training needs remains indeterminate.

Indeed, evidence from the 'Working with Bilingual Children' project suggested that the practice of the 20 LEAs which participated in the project continued to be relatively unaffected by the policy statements of Bullock, Cox and Kingman, regarding language awareness, multilingualism and related issues. Nevertheless, the project also revealed that, in principle, there was considerable support amongst educators for schemes which would enhance their understanding of these recommendations and how they might be implemented in the classroom. For a detailed outline of the 'Working with Bilingual Children' project and a discussion of its findings, see the following publications: Corrigan *et al.* (forthcoming), and Verma *et al.* (1992, 1993a, 1993b, forthcoming).

In this volume we have included contributions which reflect the views of experienced practitioners, as well as advisers and teacher-trainers engaged in curriculum development and training to meet the needs of the bilingual child. The topics include pedagogical matters such as analysing bilingual children's discourse; assessing their linguistic and conceptual competence; and the use of 'story' as vehicle. Practical matters are also discussed, such as helping children settle down in a new environment where there is very little opportunity to communicate in a shared language, as are more wide-ranging issues like monitoring equality in the classroom. The chapter on 'Issues in the Language Education of Bilingual Children' demonstrates the strength of feeling and the commitment towards bilingual children's education expressed by all participants.

This volume has been compiled for everyone interested in supporting bilingual children to develop their potential and compete on equal terms with other children. We hope this collection will be received as a contribution to the field of applied linguistics which is teacher-focused. We should like to thank all our colleagues in schools and LEAs whose help has been invaluable.

References

Bourne, J. (1989) *Moving into the Mainstream: LEA Provision for Bilingual Pupils.* Windsor: NFER-Nelson.

Brumfitt, C. (ed.) (1988) *Language in Teacher Training.* Brighton: National Congress on Language in Education. Language Centre, Brighton Polytechnic.

Carter, R.A. (ed.) (1992) *Knowledge about Language and the Curriculum: The LINC Reader.* London: Hodder & Stoughton.

Corrigan, K.P., Firth, S.A. and Verma, M.K. (forthcoming) Bilingual children in British primary schools: 'Equal but different' — Herodotus. *York Research Papers in Linguistics.* York: Department of Language and Linguistic Science, University of York.

Department of Education and Science. (1967) *Children and their Primary Schools*

(The Plowden Report). London: HMSO.

—(1975) *A Language for Life* (The Bullock Report). London: HMSO.

—(1985) *Education for All* (The Swann Report). London: HMSO.

—(1988) *Report of the Committee of Inquiry into the Teaching of English Language* (The Kingman Report). London: HMSO.

—(1989) *English for Ages 5 to 16* (The Cox Report). London: HMSO.

—(1981) *West Indian Children in our Schools* (Rampton Committee). London: HMSO.

Verma, M.K., Corrigan, K.P. and Firth, S.A. (1992) The developing phonological system of Panjabi/Urdu speaking children learning English as a second language in Britain. In J. Leather and J. Allen (eds) *New Sounds 1992: Proceedings of the 1992 Amsterdam Symposium on the Acquisition of Second-language Speech.* Amsterdam: University of Amsterdam.

—(1993a) *Working with Bilingual Children: Final Report to Humberside Local Education Authority.* York: Department of Language and Linguistic Science, University of York.

—(1993b) *Working with Bilingual Children: Final Report to University Funding Council.* York: Department of Language and Linguistic Science, University of York.

—(forthcoming) Minority children's heritage language: Planning for non-preservation? In P. Wynn-Thomas (ed.) *Proceedings of the Fifth International Conference on Minority Languages.* Cardiff: University of Wales Press.

Contributors

Lindy Bates:	Independent Literacy Consultant, Postgraduate Researcher in Bilingualism, Kent.
Karen P. Corrigan:	Lecturer in English Language and Linguistics, University of Newcastle-upon-Tyne.
Sally Firth:	Researcher, 'Working with Bilingual Children Project', University of York.
Ola Francombe:	ESL Co-ordinator, Northamptonshire Multicultural Education Service.
Edie Garvie:	Consultant, Multicultural Education.
Nanette Godfrey:	ESL Language Support Service, Birmingham.
Ann Hindle:	Head ESL Service (schools), Lothian Region.
Jean Mills:	Senior Lecturer, Westhill College, Birmingham.
Mary Rose Peate:	Postgraduate Researcher and ESL Teacher, University of Wales College of Cardiff.
William H. Raybould:	Director of Welsh Language Education Development Committee.
Ann Robson:	Senior Educational Psychologist, London Borough of Wandsworth.
Silvia Skinner:	ESL Language Support Service, Birmingham.
Farzana Turner:	General Education Inspector Multicultural, Northamptonshire.
Mahendra K. Verma:	Lecturer in Hindi and Linguistics, University of York.

1 Investigating Children's Discourse in the Primary Classroom: The Linguistic Demands of Classroom Tasks

NANETTE GODFREY and SILVIA SKINNER

This paper describes current classroom research into children's discourse being carried out in primary schools by ESL teachers in Birmingham, as part of their professional development programme. The purpose of the research is to examine, through discourse analysis, how fluent English-speaking children respond to the linguistic demands of the National Curriculum, so that information obtained can be used to shape English-teaching programmes which will increase access to the curriculum for developing-bilingual pupils. The paper tells how the research was prompted by ESL teachers studying a theory of second language acquisition and bilingual development, and using a bilingual teaching methodology based on it. An account is given of the most recent stage of the research project – an investigation into the way linguistic demands can vary within a curriculum task. It is illustrated by work carried out by the ESL teachers in one school.

Introduction

The following is an account of work which grew out of the study and use by the Primary ESL Unit in Birmingham of the bilingual method of teaching a language, devised and developed by Carl Dodson. Dodson's theory and methodology (1985a & b) derive from his own clearly-recalled experience of learning a second language at the age of 15, and his experience within three years of that of finding himself in the position of teaching his own first language of acquisition to others. He recalls that the direct method he was expected to use in his teaching bore no relationship to the processes he vividly remembered himself using when he was learning his second language. Many years later it came about that he had

1

the chance to test his own language teaching ideas and incorporate them in his bilingual methodology.

The direct method uses the natural language acquisition process of a young child as a model on which to base second language teaching practice and makes the assumption, therefore, that second language learners acquire their second language in the same way as they acquired their first. Dodson, however, believes that an additional language is acquired differently from the way monolinguals learn their only language, or bilinguals a first in any area of experience, and he carefully analyses the role that he sees the stronger language playing in the acquisition of the second. Having rejected terms such as *first* or *dominant language* and *mother tongue* as inexplicit and imprecise, he defines the stronger language carefully and introduces the idea of *preferred language* (which he calls a neutral psychological term like 'preferred image' in the field of perception) as the language in which a bilingual finds it easier to make any utterances in any area of experience at any given time. Preferred language does not indicate a preference for, or a wish to use a particular language, and he stresses the criterion of 'ease of use' which can be affected by social, psychological and other factors as well as the level of language proficiency.

He also differentiates between two types of communicative utterances in first and second language acquisition, drawing on recorded evidence of children's speech activities, particularly that of Weir (1962), who noticed that her young monolingual son's pre-sleep monologues consisted of two types of talk. At times the child appeared to play with language, reminding her of her own direct method teaching activities, and at other times he communicated with toys and imaginary people, his mind at these moments clearly focused on the messages he was sending. Dodson develops this idea and refers to the process where the speaker focuses on the language as medium-orientated communication and where the speaker focuses on the message as message-orientated communication. He points out that any utterance can be totally medium-orientated or totally message-orientated or a mixture of both, depending on the speech intentions of the speaker. Dodson emphasises that both levels of activity and the fluctuating process between them are essential for successful language learning and the achievement of balanced bilingualism.

He then examines the language-learning process of young children focusing on the strategies they use in medium-orientated private speech. He describes how both monolinguals and bilinguals use the same four monolingual strategies when learning their only or first language. They imitate utterances they have heard someone else say; they create new utterances by substituting different elements; they add new known elements to extend the meaning and they chain together known utterances to produce a flow of speech. However, when bilinguals are learning their second language they use two additional strategies only available to those who speak a second language, strategies that are deliberately excluded from direct method teaching. They compare and contrast utterances from both languages and use their preferred language to seek the meaning of unfamiliar words and sentences in their second language. In other words, in acquiring a second language, a developing-bilingual's total linguistic activity can be seen as a fluctuating process between bilingual medium-orientated communication and monolingual message-orientated communication. As proficiency in the second language increases, the need for prior bilingual medium-orientated communication decreases. It should be noted, however, that even for balanced bilinguals it never entirely disappears.

Dodson sums up his theory thus:

> all developing and developed bilinguals, no matter what their age or environment, have a preferred and a second language, specific and general, and ... a developing bilingual increases his competence in his second language through an overall fluctuating activity between bilingual preferred/second-language medium-orientated communication and monolingual second-language message-orientated communication, with the former decreasing in inverse proportion to his increasing proficiency in the second language. Both communicative levels are essential and one without the other will handicap the bilingual, whether developing or developed, in his efforts to become, or remain, a balanced bilingual. (1985b: 339)

The preceding description of Dodson's bilingual development theory is cursory and a full account of the theoretical framework can be found in his 'Second language acquisition and bilingual development: A theoretical framework' (1985b). There are full details and explanations of the steps and stages of the methodology based on the theory in *Bilingual Education: Evaluation, Assessment and Methodology* (Dodson, 1985a). It must be stressed that, although the approach is ordered and structured, the method is extremely flexible for use in the classroom and adapts to many different situations.

This theory was the stimulus for the classroom research programmes which were carried out by newly appointed teachers as part of their two-year initial training course in the Primary ESL Unit. A feature of the use of the bilingual method which ESL and mainstream teachers have found particularly beneficial for developing-bilingual children is the way in which bilingual medium-orientated communication is linked to the monolingual message-orientated communication, which in their case is the language of the classroom. This gives potential for accelerating children's acquisition of English and for enabling children to have more rapid access to curriculum activities.

However, there is a crucial stage of preparation to be undertaken by teachers before they start the cycle of lessons which will take the children from medium into message-orientated communication for any given activity. Their planning must begin at the point where, in the lesson cycle, they expect the children to finish – at the activity itself. It is here that specific information must be gathered about the linguistic demands the activity makes, and about the linguistic strategies fluent English-speaking children use to meet these demands. It was to give the ESL teachers the opportunity to investigate this that the research programmes were introduced.

In-service Training: The Research Programme

The focus now turns to the rationale behind the in-service training programme which grew from the needs of the Primary ESL teachers as they were developing the use of the bilingual method. The method requires teachers to have a detailed and clear understanding of children's communicative interactions in the learning activities of the classroom, and it was for this reason that programmes of professional development within the unit ventured into the realms of linguistic research and discourse analysis. The research was also in accord with the philosophy adopted by the Primary ESL management in all its professional education programmes (Skinner, 1992) that reflective, enquiry-based approaches to practice, supported by planned and researched in-service training can have positive outcomes for the professional development of teachers (Stenhouse, 1975; Elliott, 1976; Hopkins, 1985; Walker, 1985).

A survey of terms which make reference to oral communication within the attainment targets of the National Curriculum was carried out by the teacher research groups at the start of the work. It revealed that an amazingly wide variety of styles of discourse was demanded of children in their curriculum tasks (Primary ESL, 1990a: 4). This led the ESL teachers to consider how they could help their developing-bilingual pupils to meet these linguistic demands. Thus began four years of projects in which groups of primary ESL teachers taped, transcribed and analysed samples of everyday classroom discourse in their schools. The in-service projects took the form of co-ordinated programmes, with teachers working in their schools on the same specific area of linguistic investigation and coming back to their weekly in-service meetings to share their findings. The work was centred on the premise that, since the aim was to use the bilingual method to enable pupils to acquire English and at the same time have rapid access to the curriculum, language used for teaching purposes must be based on the curriculum and immediately accessible and useful to pupils.

Reference was made above to Dodson's theory that language learners need constantly to fluctuate between medium- and message-orientated communication. However, he maintains that, although both levels are vital to the second language learning process, 'only one of these levels gives pupils a real opportunity to reach communicative competence'. His concern is that too great a proportion of language teaching remains at the first level and the process 'does not often progress into the higher communicative levels where communicative competence can flourish. Hence many teachers are faced with the constant struggle of creating classroom situations which ... do not bring their pupils to a stage where they can handle language in truly communicative acts' (1985a: 162). In situations where pupils need to be sufficiently bilingual to cope with the daily interactions of school this has particular implications for the language support provided. Dodson contends that it is not medium-orientated communication alone but the constant linking of the two levels within cycles of teaching which will lead pupils to become 'lost' in the content (the message) and to become less and less aware of form (the medium): 'Without switching the pupil from the medium to the message we shall tread water for ever' (1985a: 179).

The important preparatory stage for ESL teachers in lesson planning cycles has already been mentioned. The curriculum activity having been identified, they must assess (a) whether their pupils can tackle the activity directly in English, (b) whether at their stage of development in English it would be more appropriate that the classroom organisation, if possible, should allow them to go forward in their preferred language, or (c) whether, with bilingual medium-orientated rehearsal to prepare them for the task, they would succeed in English. Whatever the answer, the teacher must think carefully about the linguistic demands of the task, but if the answer is (c), a stage of observation, recording and analysis then begins in order to identify those utterances which will give pupils access to that activity. This stage is crucial if children are to develop communication skills which are of immediate impact for their learning in the classroom.

It should be noted at this point that, in this article, the role of the preferred language in the acquisition of English is being addressed, not bilingual education or the role of ethnic minority languages in the education of ethnic minority children. It was to provide support for the development of language-teaching programmes being carried out by ESL teachers using the bilingual method in their primary classrooms, and to try to develop a common core of information about discourse styles, common utterances and key utterances used in curriculum tasks, that Primary ESL chose this area of linguistic research.

Since the research groups were looking at the acquisition of English as a second language, they concentrated their study on the interactions of children who were fluent and confident speakers of English. How did they organise their discourse to cope with particular learning activities in the classroom? It was felt that any information which could be gained about the strategies these children used in carrying out their learning tasks would enable teachers to assess how to provide language teaching programmes for pupils who were still developing their English. It should be made clear that, in doing this, assumptions were being made about a norm in the identification of fluent speakers of English. Such assumptions, of course, are fraught with difficulties and inconsistencies. How can one say what is the norm in terms of fluency in any language? However, it was felt that since the aim of the in-service training project was to enable teachers to think more analytically about the immediate and long-term linguistic needs of their developing-bilingual pupils, research into the linguistic behaviour of children who were generally agreed by their teachers to be fluent speakers of English and who were using English confidently and successfully in tackling classroom learning objectives, could reveal useful information about the linguistic and learning needs of children who have to operate in the classroom in a language in which they are not yet fluent and with which they are probably not very comfortable.

The questions explored, therefore, were:

What linguistic demands are made on young speakers of English by certain curriculum activities within the primary classroom?

What type of discourse is generated by a particular activity (or part of an activity)?

Are there high frequency utterances which recur again and again across a range of activities – and why is this?

Which key utterances, though not recurring with a noticeable regularity, stand out as crucial and essential in terms of giving access to a particular activity?

By trying to find answers to these questions, the research groups sought to build up a picture of the discourse generated by curriculum activities presented to children in the classroom.

The work proved to be valuable in terms of professional development within the unit. It increased understanding of how children use talk to get things done, how they communicate their curricular needs and how they achieve their aims in the classroom. Insights gained by the teachers in their individual schools were shared within the in-service groups, and had an immediacy and an impact. Work was always carefully planned, monitored, documented and evaluated. The findings of one research project frequently acted as the starting point for another and, because linguistic research into child discourse became a central element of in-service training programmes for the ESL teachers, the development of new understandings and knowledge was incremental. It was found that, by sharing and comparing findings, patterns of similarity emerged and a small, but cumulative bank of information began to develop. As the work developed, the research projects went into other more specific areas of child discourse in the classroom. Although the linguistic projects formed part of the two-year initial-training course for ESL teachers newly appointed to the unit, they did not repeat the same themes. Rather, work already completed became course material for future courses, and teachers were given the opportunity to go forward into other areas of investigation from the ground already gained.

The Project: Investigating Children's Discourse in the Primary Classroom

The preceding comments on the research programme which focused on giving developing-bilingual pupils access to the curriculum through meeting the linguistic demands of classroom tasks, will now be illustrated by describing in some detail a current project. As much data from the project have yet to be analysed at this stage, only the findings of one particular partnership will be examined. The project was planned to enable those taking part to gain insights into child interaction in the classroom and into the linguistic demands made on children at different stages of an activity designed to satisfy attainment targets within the National Curriculum. The research was carried out in 12 primary schools, thus enabling comparison of results across a sample of 12 sets of data. The sets of tapes and transcripts produced by the 12 research pairs covered a range of attainment targets and a variety of tasks including, for example, a co-operative investigation of the value of a pulley system (technology), planning and designing a map for visitors to school (geography), and discussing and choosing five objects from the present day to put into a time capsule (history).

The teachers who took part in the project were all in their second year of the two-year initial-training programme. The theory component of the course had included a language study module in which the teachers studied discourse analysis and theories of discourse (e.g. text construction and cohesion, Halliday & Hasan, 1976; language functions, Halliday, 1975; conversational principles, Grice, 1975; speech act theory, Austin, 1962 and Searle, 1969; conversational analysis, Levinson, 1983; and theories of discourse, Cook, 1989). As a result, they were aware of research in the field and were able to draw on this in working out their own approaches to analysis for the purposes of their own project. They also had experience of carrying out linguistic research in two previous projects. In the first of these they had investigated the linguistic demands made by collaborative problem-solving activities within the attainment targets of the science curriculum, and in the second they had looked at the demands of connected narrative discourse. Consequently, before they embarked on this investigation, they had to a great extent overcome the problems that can beset first attempts to tape and observe children's interactions.

Research which the teachers found helpful in terms of analysing pupils' discourse in curriculum tasks was fairly wide-ranging, and included, in particular, research into second language acquisition and work on high frequency communicative acts (Dodson, 1985a); research into communicative proficiency – especially the linguistic demands of classroom interactions and the role of primary language development in promoting educational success for language students (Cummins, 1981, 1983, 1984); styles of teacher/pupil discourse in whole class discussion (Sinclair and Coulthard, 1975); research on group interaction in the classroom – especially work on linguistic features indicating co-operation and the tentative nature of exploratory talk (Barnes & Todd, 1977); work on linguistic markers in children's classroom discourse – especially discourse styles in children's talk (Phillips, 1985); and work on turn-taking in conversational discourse (Sacks et al., 1974).

Since the purpose of the project was to allow teachers to investigate the immediacy and variability of linguistic demand which may be made on pupils even within one curriculum task, and to enable them to tailor their language teaching to the changing linguistic demands with which their developing-bilingual pupils were continually being confronted, this study drew particularly on two pieces of research: (1) Dodson's theory of second language acquisition and bilingual education outlined above, especially high frequency speech patterns (Dodson, 1985a: 166); and (2) Cummins' work on the linguistic demands of the classroom in which his theory suggests two dimensions of language proficiency relating to the degree of contextual support available to the pupil in classroom interactions. He proposes that in *context-embedded* communication verbal and non-verbal cues give access to understanding and support communication, whereas in *context-reduced* communication there are few cues (see Cummins, 1981; also, for an overview of Cummins' research see Baker, 1988: 174–81).

The overall aim of the investigation, therefore, was to examine the linguistic skills children need to engage in context-embedded and context-reduced communication in the primary classroom and to consider the implications for developing-bilingual children and ESL teaching. The investigation followed the established pattern of the previous exercises in that it was carried out in pairs in the school where one of the two partners was normally based and the aims, purpose and organisation of the project had been discussed with the head-teacher. The host ESL teacher was responsible for liaising with the class teacher and selecting children who were fluent and confident speakers of English and who were likely to co-operate well, while the visiting ESL teacher was responsible for organising and overseeing the taping.

The task set was to devise an activity with their mainstream colleague, relating to the history, geography or technology curriculum if possible, and to tape the selected pupils as the lesson passed through three different phases, namely: listening to the teacher's instructions; carrying out the activity (designed to promote context-embedded communication); and reporting back to an appropriate audience (or some other such process involving context-reduced communication, e.g. describing or explaining). In order to record as complete a picture as possible, the teachers were asked to make notes during their observation periods on such things as the level of involvement, initiative-taking, co-operation and non-verbal communication. Organisational guidelines were given to the staff at the beginning of the project. Additional guidelines were produced at three later stages to provide further support to the teachers in: the collection of data; the transcription and analysis of data; and the production of their presentation to other colleagues. The guidelines given to the teachers as they began their investigations were specific and were to be used by everyone so that there would be a unified approach to the collection of linguistic data, and so that the findings could be analysed across the sample as well as for individual schools.

Because of previous Primary ESL investigations into conversational and narrative discourse styles in curriculum tasks, and because communication at this stage had, for the purposes of the investigation, been intentionally designed to be context-embedded, the teachers expected to find that the second stage would make more limited linguistic demands on the children. They anticipated, too, that the third stage would make considerable linguistic demands on the children because it was to be context-reduced in structure. The demands of stage 1, however, were less clearly defined. For example, in circumstances where insufficient contextual support was provided by teachers, children could find listening to and interpreting the information needed for their task quite difficult. Where teachers were sensitive to pupils' linguistic needs and monitored their understanding, the communication produced could become more context-embedded and more easily understood. In their observation and reporting of stage 1, therefore, teachers were asked to consider their own talk, the type of discourse this part of the task produced, and the nature and level of the linguistic demands it made on the children.

Two ESL teachers worked on a technology task (Attainment Target 3 Levels 1 & 2) and linked their work to *The Gingerbread Man*, a story which fitted in with the class topic, Journeys. The children with whom they worked consisted of three fluent seven-year-old English speakers from year 2, a girl (S) and a boy (H), both balanced bilinguals (Panjabi/English), and a boy (R) who was a monolingual English speaker. The task was designed to cover all three stages of the project. At stage 1 the children were told the story and asked to design and construct a craft to take the gingerbread man over the river so that he would not be eaten by the fox. To satisfy the context-embedded section of the project (stage 2), the children were to work co-operatively with a range of junk materials to plan and construct the craft. Finally, they were to describe what they had done by making an explanatory tape for the visiting ESL teacher to take back to play to her pupils. This was to be the third stage where there would be less contextual support or cues to aid their discourse and where they would have to rely on their own linguistic resources to carry them through.

The Project: The Linguistic Demands of Stage 1

The aim of this part of the investigation was to gain insights into the way children met the linguistic demands of the teachers' introduction.

Did they use identifiable strategies to gain access to understanding? If so, what were they? Because of the degree of linguistic demand made in listening to and interpreting the discourse, teachers were asked to note the extent to which they themselves tended towards a context-embedded form of communication during this stage, even though they were working with fluent speakers of English.

In all 12 studies it had been agreed that this stage would incorporate a set of instructions which would be carried out by the children later, in stage 2. In the gingerbread man study the instructions were preceded by a narrative. Although the introduction appeared to be highly contextualised in a story which was well known to the children, and supported by text and pictures, digesting the instructions seem to have proved more difficult, perhaps because there was insufficient contextual support. The children listened attentively to the story, which was one of their favourites, but the teachers later found that there was a carry-over of misunderstanding into stage 2. One child thought the instruction 'make a tape' meant that he was to construct a tape-recorder and in one part of the interaction (not transcribed) he keeps repeating 'We need some metal'. Moreover, although the children had been told to work together on one model, they started off by making individual models. The teachers had to give a considerable amount of support in terms of checking understanding and explaining at the second stage before the group began to work co-operatively and on task. It is worth noting the teachers' comment that, after they had explained the task, the children had not sought to negotiate meaning but had immediately started work without asking questions or seeking any further interaction with them.

The Project: The Linguistic Demands of Stage 2

The activity for the second stage of the task had been designed by the ESL teachers to give the children's communication a high level of contextual support. The aims now were to identify the linguistic demands of this new stage, to investigate the skills and strategies used by their fluent English-speaking pupils in tackling these demands, and to identify which contextual elements of the activity were providing support. At this point it may be helpful to look at a section transcribed by the two teachers.

Transcript 1: *A Technology Task* (AT3, 1 & 2)
Children: Sara – Harjit – Rikki (7 years). The children's names have been changed.

H: I know.

S: I can make it like this.

H: Let's make a long one.

R: I am going to make one. I will start one.

5 H: Rikki. Rikki.

R: I know (picks up a large polythene box).

(Teacher. Do you think it will fit in the river?)

R: I think it's too big.

H: Yeah. Let's cut this corner.... need the glue.

10 (Sara working on her own)

R: We have to cut it. Let's make a small one.

H: Yeah.

H: Yeah (chooses another box), if it didn't float... in the water....

15 R: I think I know.

(Harjit starts making 'cork people' and leaves Rikki to make the boat)

H: Is the hole all right, Rikki? Rikki, is the hole all right? What do you think? I am just going to make the hole (for

20 arms), all right Rikki? (giggles) Rikki.... just going to put the hole....

R: OK man.

(Sara joins in)

S: Are we going to need this or not?

25 R: What's that?

S: Flag.

H: What's this?

S: Put this inside.

H: It's a good idea to put this inside.

30 S: Let me do something.

H: It might not stick.

S: I will glue it, OK?.... There are some seats.

R: There's only three seats.

H: It won't have space to put this....

35 S: I will squeeze it for you Rikki.

R: That's enough.

S: Yeah, all right.

H: Do you think it will fit?

R: I don't know.

40 H: How do you stick it?

S: What are we going to do?

H: How are we going to get the boat from this side to that?

R: Blow it.

S: Push it.

45 R: Don't bother.

S: I will get the water.

In their analysis the teachers were asked to consider how the structure they had devised for their activity might have provided support for the children's communication. In previous projects it had been found that certain tasks which involved a repetitive 'testing' process, such as classifying a collection of objects or materials according to certain properties, for example by weight, texture, etc. were accompanied by a matching pattern of talk between the children, with repeated utterances and sequences of utterances which reflected the structure of the activity. These tasks had been found to be less linguistically demanding than open-ended tasks, and helpful in giving access to the curriculum to early developing-bilingual pupils (Primary ESL, 1990a & b). Analysis of the boat-building activity chosen by the teachers in the gingerbread man activity seems to show that it was less 'closed' than the examples given above. However, although it was not repetitive in the same way, since the teachers allowed choice for the children to take their own path to the final objective, it is possible to identify features which may have been influenced by the demands and structure of the activity. These help to build up a picture of the linguistic framework within which the children were operating.

For example, it was expected that as the children worked and talked together in their groups they would supplement their verbal communication by touching or pointing to the materials. Throughout the gingerbread man activity the children constantly used deictic (pointing) expressions in the form of personal or demonstrative pronouns to denote objects and position, e.g.: 'I can make it like this.' (line 2); 'It won't have space to put this.' (line 34); 'There are some seats.' (line 32). This allowed them to link their discourse to the context. It is a repetitive and economical form of communication and appears to have helped the children to continue their talk, reducing the level of linguistic demand made on them.

The teachers were asked to analyse in terms of high frequency utterances – another form of linguistic repetition directly related to the structure of the activity. Deictic expressions have already been mentioned as having a high frequency in the gingerbread man interaction. The same applies to the use of utterances relating to the *personal* language function (Halliday, 1975), e.g. 'I know.' (lines 1 and 6); 'I think I know.' (line 15; see also lines 8, 32, 35 and 46), and the *interactional* language function e.g. 'Let's make a long one'(line 3); 'Let's cut this corner' (line 9; see also lines 11, 30 and 42). There is also a high frequency of utterances using the future of intention e.g. 'I'm just going to make the hole .... just going to put the hole' (lines 19; see also lines 4, 24, 41 and 42).

The teachers also analysed the interaction to identify key utterances. Although these utterances are crucial for carrying out an activity, they do not necessarily have a particularly high frequency. In the case of the gingerbread man transcript, however, some of the high frequency utterances are also key utterances. The discourse shows that, in tackling the linguistic demands of their technology task, all three children found it important to use: (1) utterances relating to their own needs so that they could hold their own in the interaction; (2) utterances relating to co-operation, to satisfy the collaborative aspects of the activity, and (3) utterances relating to information about what they intended to do (future of intention), especially as in line 42 'How are we going to....?' with substitutions of various key verbs and phrases relating to their model making (e.g. make/cut/glue, etc.).

A major element of the context-embedded nature of stage 2 was to be the support provided by the children to each other as they worked together. Teachers expected this to help communication and reduce the level of linguistic demand made by the activity. Throughout the section transcribed here, there are features in the children's discourse which show co-operation. The frequent use of 'let's' and 'we' indicates shared action. Their talk contains a number of questions denoting attention to each other's opinions (lines 18, 31 – 32, etc.). It contains cohesive markers between the turns from one child to another, indicating a readiness to listen and acknowledge each other's contributions e.g. 'Yeah.' (line 9); 'What do you think?' (lines 18 – 19); 'OK man.' (line 22); 'Yeah all right.' (line 37). The interaction appears informal, relaxed and supportive.

A closer look at the distribution of turns, however, shows that the talk tended to be mostly between H and R, and that S, the only girl, seemed to find the situation quite demanding because of her difficulty in gaining entry to the discussion. She used a variety of strategies in her attempt to enter the discussion and hold her own in the group (see lines 2, 24, 26, 28), resorting in line 30 to a direct 'Let me do something'. She succeeded in the end (lines 30–46) – a gender issue, or just the fact that H and R were very good friends?

Since one of the objectives of this investigation was to discover which aspects of the whole task made considerable linguistic demands and which did not, the teachers were also asked to consider where, on a linguistic continuum between formal discourse and spontaneous conversation, the second stage lay. For example, the gingerbread man interaction has many of the features of spontaneous conversation. There is a tentativeness in the discourse, with its brief, often unfinished utterances. There is evidence of a regard for conversational principles in, for example, the way children use language for maintaining social contact ('All right?', 'OK man.'). However, it is interesting to note the suggestion made by some linguists that talk cannot be classed as conversation if it is primarily necessitated by a practical task (Cook, 1989: 51). Analysis of the discourse in the gingerbread man transcript seems to suggest that, although at first it appears unstructured and unpredictable, this is not the open-endedness of spontaneous conversation. Because the children remain 'on task', their talk is constantly directed towards the activity and does not move at random to other topics. This stage clearly made demands on the speakers to use language in certain ways. However, it is suggested that these demands were fairly limited because of the dual support derived from the conversational informality of the talk and the practical nature of the activity.

The Project: The Linguistic Demands of Stage 3

The children now had to be able to adapt their discourse to a new set of linguistic demands. They were to be involved in a context-reduced form of communication based on recall of their practical activity. This was to be in the form of a report, description or explanation. In analysing this stage the teachers were asked to investigate the effect that the reduced level of contextual support was having on the children's discourse, and the way individual children tackled the linguistic demands of the activity. The children working on the gingerbread man activity recorded their report on tape (transcript 2). Perhaps a look at their performance will give some indication of the linguistic demands of this stage and the linguistic resources the children drew on to tackle them.

Transcript 2: *A Technology Task* (AT 3, 1 & 2)
Children: Sara – Harjit – Rikki (7 years). The children's names have been changed.

R: First of all Mrs K— read a story to us and we had to solve a problem for the gingerbread man to get across the river. So, first we made a boat and we decorated it.... we put some people in and then we tried to.... and we put

5   a flag on it and then we tried.... um.... floated it for it didn't work. So we made the big (fairy/ferry?) one and then.... and then the gingerbread man.... um.... he could sit.... er.... sit on the chair and then there's a dustbin there and then.... (whispers

to others). Your turn.... say

10   it.... say something....

S: First Mrs K— read us a story. Then we made a boat and the
     gingerbread man was in there and when we floated it.... the head
     went down.... it was wet and we made a more better one and
     that was working.... was a big

15   one.... plastic things.

R: And we used boxes and a bit of paper and beads and we made a
     big one with a big toilet roll, and then we made another
     gingerbread man because that other one was soaked from the
     water and then we floated it and then we found out that

20   that one worked better.

H: When we made the first boat, we used [whispering] corks and
     um.... we made a flag [whispering].... we used the beads and
     we made the flag and we made the men and we put them....
     inside the boat and we tried it in the tub. It

25   didn't work.... [whispering].

R: Then we.... another. We made a good one then [whispering] the
     yoghurt pot.... a big toilet roll ....and we used the beads to make
     a dustbin.

A comparison of the two transcripts shows that at this stage the
children needed to be more self-sufficient in their contributions, to rely
on the spoken word alone, and to be able to use longer stretches of
connected discourse. In the second transcript it will be seen that,
although all three children managed to sustain a reasonable stretch of
connected talk in their first turn, at the end of the turn the account tended
to tail off. The effort of maintaining the momentum of this type of
communication clearly appeared to make considerable demands on the
speakers, particularly on R: 'Your turn.... say it.... say something....'
(lines 9–10).

Part of the increased level of linguistic demand made on speakers in
context-reduced situations may arise from the need to shape and
organise longer stretches of discourse. The teachers, therefore, analysed
their transcripts in terms of particular linguistic items used by their
pupils in organising and sequencing facts and events. Analysis shows
that time and time-sequence were significant for reporting the activity. In
terms of organisation, therefore, the children had to be able to handle
past tenses and to select and use appropriate ways of marking
chronological sequence. They also had to give their account a beginning,
a middle and an end. Both R and S managed this efficiently, giving the

main events of the boat-building activity in a chronological sequence. They opened in an appropriate way (S: 'First Mrs K— read us a story.' (line 11)), proceeded through the important points in logical sequence, and concluded (R: 'and then we found out that that one worked better.' (lines 19—20)). H had an effective opening and closing strategy but chose to give an inventory of the objects they had made for the boat rather than a sequence of events (lines 21–25).

The guidelines suggested analysis in terms of cohesion and linking across the discourse. It is noticeable that here the children used simple conjunctions to sequence and link their narrative. For the most part this took the form of clause-chaining using the connectives 'first', 'so', 'and' and 'then' as time-sequence markers. There is one example of causal chaining, R: '... and 'then we made another gingerbread man because that other one was soaked...' (lines 17–19), and two examples where S and H used a more complex subordinate clause with 'when' (lines 12 and 21). In his second and third turns R used the cohesive devices 'and' and 'then' to link neatly in to where the previous speaker had left off (lines 16 and 26).

It was suggested that, because these were oral accounts, the speakers had to be aware of the needs of the listener in judging how they imparted their information, in monitoring whether understanding had taken place and in using strategies to hold the attention. It is interesting to compare how the three children handled this. For example, in his first turn R had difficulty in meeting these demands. He gave more detail than he needed, which took him away from the main points and the account ended with unconnected and what appears to be superfluous information (line 8). As his discourse tailed off he used certain stalling devices to hold on to the turn and keep the listener's attention ('um'/'er' and repetition of 'sit' in lines 5–8). In his second turn he continued where S stopped and successfully concluded his account (lines 16–20). At first glance, H's account does not seem to stand on its own as a sequential report of the events, but in the light of the order of speaking (he took the third turn), and of the information which had already been given in the other reports, it had the effect of supplementing what the others had said (lines 21–25). S was more economical in the amount of information she gave but she got further on in her sequence at the first attempt. She selected the important facts, sequenced them and successfully concluded her report.

It would seem that, although these children handled the task well, this form of communication can make considerable linguistic demands even of the young fluent speaker of English. Part of this burden may come from the fact that such an activity may happen in circumstances of spontaneity. The fact that these children were using a tape-recorder, perhaps allowing a certain amount of 'rehearsing', may have helped the final shape of their discourse.

Conclusion

The purpose of the preceding account has been to describe how study of Dodson's theory of bilingual development and use of his bilingual method of teaching a language by teachers in the Primary ESL unit in Birmingham had the effect of stimulating a programme of classroom linguistic research. It has shown how, because of the fluctuating process in the method between medium- and message-orientated communication as learners move towards communicative competence in English, precise information was needed by the ESL teachers about the linguistic demands made on pupils by the various areas of the curriculum; how, in order to help their developing-bilingual pupils to have rapid access to the curriculum, they also needed to investigate the strategies used by young fluent English speakers to meet these demands in everyday curriculum tasks; and how these needs led to the shaping of specific research questions which the ESL teachers, in their in-service groups, attempted to answer by observing the interactions of children and collecting data in their own schools.

Central to the account has been a description of one of these research projects, where the teachers looked at the effects on children of the way the degree of linguistic demand could change across the three stages of one curriculum task. The project drew on ideas contained in Cummins' theory of context-embedded and context-reduced communication in the classroom. The account was illustrated with extracts from the taped interactions of children in one of the 12 project schools.

Analysis of all the data from the sample of 12 schools has not been completed and so it is not yet possible to report on the final results and findings of the project, nor is it possible to draw implications of the findings in the light of information already gained from previous projects. However, the case study used within this account shows that analysis of the experience of one group alone has provided insights which may have helped the teachers to answer some of the questions they were asking. They found that the linguistic demands of their classroom task changed, not only across the different stages but also within one stage; that the changes made different and sometimes considerable demands on the speakers, both in the types of discourse required and the language skills they needed to meet them. Looked at in the light of Cummins' theory, it seemed that the support within the context may have been significant in lessening these linguistic demands. For example, the stand-alone demands of having to speak independently in report-back types of discourse may have been relieved by the way the children tended to adopt a turn-taking approach in giving their contributions. They may also have been helped by the fact that use of the tape-recorder allowed 'rehearsal' before launching into a more formal form of talk. On the other hand, however, use of the tape recorder could have had the effect of distancing the audience and taking away the possibility of contextual responses by listeners.

The account refers to the incremental nature of the classroom research carried out in Birmingham since the projects began. It is hoped that when the final analysis of this project is completed, the insights and discoveries gained will take the work a little further. However, as one question is answered others form and other research areas await attention. There is still a lot more work to be done in this area and a lot more data to be collected and analysed. It is hoped, however, that this account of work carried out by Primary ESL teachers in Birmingham will be of interest to teacher groups who may be already engaged in classroom linguistic research, and to other teachers as well, both in terms of ideas for professional development and in terms of increasing access to the curriculum for developing-bilingual children.

References

Austin, J.L. (1962) *How to do Things with Words.* Oxford: Oxford University Press.

Baker, C. (1988) *Key Issues in Bilingualism and Bilingual Education.* Clevedon: Multilingual Matters.

Barnes, D. and Todd, F. (1977) *Communication and Learning in Small Groups.* London: Routledge & Kegan Paul.

Cook, G. (1989) Discourse. In C.N. Candlin and H.G. Widdowson (eds) *Language Teaching: A Scheme for Teacher Education.* Oxford: Oxford University Press.

Cummins, J. (1981) The role of primary language development in promoting educational success for language minority students. In California State Department of Education, *Schooling and Language Minority Students. A Theoretical Framework.* Los Angeles: Evaluation, Dissemination and Assessment Center.

— (1983) Language proficiency, biliteracy and French immersion. *Canadian Journal of Education* 8 (2), 117–38.

— (1984) Wanted, a theoretical framework for relating language proficiency to academic achievement among bilingual students. In C. Rivera (ed.) *Language Proficiency and Academic Achievement.* Clevedon: Multilingual Matters.

Dodson, C.J. (ed.) (1985a) *Bilingual Education: Evaluation, Assessment and*

Methodology. Cardiff: University of Wales Press.

— (1985b), Second language acquisition and bilingual development: A theoretical framework. *Journal of Multilingual and Multicultural Development* 6 (5), 325–346.

Elliott, J. (1976) *Developing Hypotheses about Classrooms from Teachers' Practical Constructs*. Ford Teaching Project. Cambridge: Cambridge Institute of Education.

Grice, H.P. (1975) Logic and conversation. In P. Cole and J.L. Morgan (eds) *Syntax and Semantics* 3. New York: Academic Press.

Halliday, M.A.K. (1975) *Learning how to Mean: Explorations in the Development of Language*. London: Edward Arnold.

Halliday, M.A.K. and Hasan, R. (1976) *Cohesion in English*. London: Longman.

Hopkins, D. (1985) *A Teacher's Guide to Classroom Research*. Milton Keynes: Open University Press.

Levinson, S. (1983) *Pragmatics*. Cambridge: Cambridge University Press.

Phillips, T. (1985) Beyond lip service: Discourse development after the age of nine. In G. Wells and J. Nicholls (eds) *Language and Learning: An Interactional Perspective*. Falmer Press for the Open University.

Primary ESL (1990a) Investigating children's talk in collaborative problem-solving tasks within the primary curriculum part 1. Unpublished paper.

— (1990b) Investigating children's talk in collaborative problem-solving tasks within the primary curriculum part 2. Unpublished paper.

Sacks, H., Schegloff, E.A. and Jefferson, G. (1974) A simplest systematics for the organization of turn-taking in conversation. *Language* 50, 696–735.

Searle, J.R. (1969) *Speech Acts*. Cambridge: Cambridge University Press.

Sinclair, J. and Coulthard, M. (1975) *Towards an Analysis of Discourse: The English used by Teachers and Pupils*. Oxford: Oxford University Press.

Skinner, S.F. (1992) Curious about classrooms: An exploration of the theme of the teacher as researcher. MEd dissertation, University of Birmingham.

Stenhouse, L.A. (1975) *An Introduction to Curriculum Research and Development*. London: Heinemann Educational Books.

Walker, R. (1985) *Doing Research: A Handbook for Teachers*. London: Routledge.

Weir, R.H. (1962) *Language in the Crib*. The Hague: Mouton.

2 Story as Vehicle: The Making of a Kit

EDIE GARVIE

This article stresses the value of story as a learning vehicle in the primary classroom, carrying as it does issues of both content and language. It is suggested that teachers build up a bank of potential stories from which classroom narratives can be devised to suit particular pupils and needs. A series of steps is offered for the making of a story kit, bearing in mind the four modes of listening, speaking, reading and writing, and also the matter of accuracy and fluency. The story kit is as much a way of approach as a container of materials, a product pointing to process.

Story is meaning and language is its medium. The most important task of the primary teacher is helping children to mean. There is no better instrument than story for accomplishing this – not just the story told on a Friday afternoon to keep restless children quiet, but the kind which is planned and adapted as a narrative for a particular group and its needs. Much of the time an appropriate story should be presented and enjoyed and left at that. It will speak for itself. But sometimes the teacher can use it as the vehicle for all kinds of things along the learning journey. It can be the conveyor of innumerable messages, about language itself in its various uses, about the content of the curriculum in general, about what is buzzing in school and community, about folklore and traditions – one's own and those of others – and many other categories of experience. This story vehicle has an important role in the primary classroom and indeed in any classroom. But what follows is aimed particularly at teachers in the lower primary sector.

My intention is to be as practical as possible. For that purpose I shall plunge straight away into some possible steps in the making of a story kit. The ideas and the sample story with its staging-posts and follow-up song are taken from Garvie (1989).

First, catch your story. By way of introduction let me stress the value of building up a story bank. This should be done gradually over the years. It can be done by an individual teacher or a team. This is true for all the suggestions made. When I say *story* here, I mean potential story – the kind of raw data for the making of classroom narratives. Usually a story heard or read has to be adapted in some way to suit the particular pupils. Sometimes it has to be devised out of a number of 'loose' messages such as a child's news or pieces of information from various children. The teacher has to decide whether to adopt, adapt or devise. The bank should contain a mixed bag of stories from all kinds of sources, preferably across cultures and across genres. Songs, rhymes and role-plays can be exciting stories too. The teacher withdraws from the bank what might be an appropriate vehicle for her purpose of the moment. This might be, for instance, a better understanding of the life-cycle of the frog which comes into the curriculum, or it might be a language issue such as the use of certain prepositions. Whatever the objective, the teacher now sets about making her story kit. The notion of a pack or kit is not new. I simply re-visit it and offer perhaps one or two additional ideas. Here, then, is a kind of recipe for turning story into narrative for the classroom.

List Your Staging-posts (see the sample story and list of staging-posts in the Appendix)

By this I mean a précis of the main points in the story. I call them staging-posts because the term goes with the idea of a vehicle going on a journey.

Use the staging-posts for three particular purposes

(1) For presenting at different levels.
(2) For guiding you in the preparation of teaching materials.
(3) For guiding you in the 'loading' of the vehicle.

Let me elaborate. Most classes have a range of ability and sometimes not all the children can understand and enjoy what is presented, either because of boredom or because of confusion. As with other classroom activities, group-work can be used for story. So why not write (for yourself) the narrative at different levels (see part 5 of Garvie (1989) for an example of this). The practicalities in the classroom cannot be gone into here, but for the experienced primary teacher they should present no problem. What I want to concentrate on is the preparatory process. Using the staging-posts as a guideline, then, it is possible to write the narrative at different levels of complexity. It would be better done as a team activity and could be a very interesting and enlightening ploy. One of the most difficult exercises for the fluent user of a language is to write simply!

Concerning the second use of the staging-posts (the preparation of teaching materials), here again is a helpful guideline. Most teachers of young children are familiar with the need for visual and other kinds of aid and most are skilled in their devising. Let the staging-posts offer ideas, and think carefully about the kind and amount. Are they to complement or supplement the text or perhaps simply to illustrate? How much understanding can the children gain from words alone? Do the different groups need more or less by way of aids? These are important issues, completely apart from the usual ones about kind of material, size, colour of visual, etc. There could be a set of pictures, one for each staging-post for one level, and perhaps for the more able children all of these need not be used. Or again, it might be decided to illustrate only one or two of the staging-posts, using each as a kind of gathering of points as the story progresses. And of course the aids could be auditory or linked to any other sense or a mixture of senses. As you study your guideline the ideas will flow.

The third use of the staging-posts (the 'loading' of the vehicle) perhaps needs the most thought. It is here, I feel, that we so often lose opportunities. Most stories carry much more learning than the story theme. We could make more of this by pausing at particular staging-posts and, as it were, filling out the language in the story to give the meaning more exposure. For instance, at staging-post 10 in the story in the Appendix ('sees empty barrow'), the teacher could insert 'the barrow was empty – there was nothing in it' after 'his hats had gone'. That is, we could use a story even more effectively by deliberately loading in what we want the children to learn. I have referred above to the life-cycle of the frog and the use of prepositions. These are examples of concept and language learning. All stories carry both. Which items are to be focused on? Is there enough learning material as the text stands or do we need to adapt so that more emphasis is given to certain parts? For instance, in the story in the Appendix the hatmaker is looking for his hats. The teacher might want to concentrate on staging-post 11 and elaborate in the presentation. She wants to revise the prepositions *behind, in front of* and beside. So she makes the hatmaker use them and demonstrates 'behind the tree' etc. The teacher should know her children's needs so well and the syllabus/curriculum to be covered that she quickly recognises the potential of a story to be a vehicle for one or more issues of learning.

Prepare Follow-up Materials

Any story kit should contain not only the aids for the initial presentation of the story but a number of further materials so that the story learning can be generalised. For instance, see the song in the Appendix. This uses the hats from the story. Perhaps the teacher 'loaded' in the colour terms when she presented it or perhaps she discussed other articles of clothing. Songs, rhymes, games and role-plays are all useful follow-up ploys. Or if the story was one of these in the first place, then a prose version becomes part of the follow-up. And we must not forget reading and writing activities. What I have hinted at so far is oral work, the teacher telling rather than reading the story, the children acting or re-telling, using the teacher's 'scaffolding' for their own version. But out of all this meaningful oracy comes literacy. Here lies your comprehension and work-sheet, the children given perhaps the written-down text. I am not suggesting that the teacher never reads the story. This should be done as an example of what books are for but it has to be done well, the teacher not losing eye-contact with the pupils.

So in the story kit we are concerned with both oracy and literacy: listening, speaking, reading and writing. I suggest that we also be concerned with what are sometimes referred to as accuracy and fluency, the two sides of the language coin. On the one hand the pupil has to learn the rules of usage, the grammar and the spelling, and on the other, the conventions of use. What do we say to whom, when and how? Let the story help by presenting these things and the follow-up by consolidating. Let there be games for instance which demand accuracy of response and those which aim at role-playing. Again, see Garvie (1989) for further ideas. Going with the story used here there is a tense-sequencing game and a photographic bingo. The hatmaker, the monkeys and the hats continue to be used. And speaking of continuity, there could be some reference in the story kit to ways in which the story theme is to be used in other areas of the curriculum such as science and mathematics.

Prepare Extension Materials

This is really more of the same, except that the emphasis should now be on stretching the children a bit, encouraging new ideas and creative use of the earlier work. It is fun, for example, to prepare a set of 'funny visuals' based on the original story. These could range from the merely different to the incongruous. Do the children notice the differences? Is the leading character wearing something different? Does the building have more windows or a chimney missing? Or to come to the incongruous and using the hatmaker story, is the man up the tree and the monkeys on the ground? Are the monkeys replaced by elephants? Is the man taking his hats to market in a boat? Most children enjoy this kind of thing and new language can be introduced such as *instead* of. The children can be encouraged to think of their own incongruities. They could also be encouraged to re-tell the story from the point of view of a character in it. Perhaps some of the more able children could devise extensions to the story, both before and after. Where did the man make his hats and how? What went on in the market? But I stray once again into methodology.

Write Some Guidelines for the Use of your Kit

This is both as reminder to yourself and as help to anyone else who might like to use your story. The following is taken from Garvie (1989):

(1) Have an overall summary of the kit – items listed – with an introductory paragraph or so describing the rationale of the story methodology (this could be the same for all your kits with perhaps just a short particular piece added for each story).
(2) For each item in the kit there should be a brief note explaining the purpose. This should cross-reference with the overall list.
(3) Show clearly the age(s) and stage(s) of the learners the kit is intended for.
(4) State which parts of the syllabus/curriculum areas are loaded into the story.
(5) List any useful references, e.g. another story which might pick up the learning from this one.
(6) Note further ideas which could be developed. Remember that stories differ in their potential and some are better than others for carrying certain things.
(7) Be brief and to the point.

The story kit is in fact as much a way of thinking as an actual container of things – a process rather than a product. But the product is useful to point us to the process. A see-through bag for quick reference in which lie the classroom narratives at more than one level, and sets of materials for both presentation and follow-up or the reference to them and further ideas, is a useful teaching tool. But each kit must be revised from time to time as new ideas spring to mind and new needs require to be met. The bank too should be considered afresh, some items discarded and others added. Old stories die hard. At the same time, current life produces its own. So story brings us the universals and the particulars of life. Surely this is what education is all about. It is one of the reasons why some of us are seeing the value of the story-based curriculum with new eyes. But that is a story which needs further telling. Think about it.

Appendix

The Hatmaker and the Monkeys

Once upon a time in a land far away there lived a hatmaker. One day he thought that he had enough hats ready to sell so he loaded his barrow with them and set out for the market. It was a very hot day and it was a long journey. The man began to feel very tired. He came to a tree with spreading branches. He was pleased to sit down under it in the shade. Soon he was fast asleep. He did not know that there were monkeys up in the tree. They wanted to learn more about those hats. After the man was sound asleep they crept down the tree and took the hats out of the barrow. Each put one on and then they all climbed back to their places in the branches.

After a while the hatmaker woke up. He soon knew that something was different. His hats had gone. Where could they be? He looked all over the place and at last he looked up into the tree. There were the monkeys sitting with the hats on. They seemed happy. The hatmaker was very angry. He scowled and shook his fist. Perhaps the monkeys scowled too. But they did shake their fists. Monkeys can imitate well. They copy the things people do. The hatmaker had an idea. He would get them to copy him again. He took off his hat and threw it on the ground. Then he waited to see what would happen. His idea worked. The monkeys did the same. So the hatmaker got his hats back. He did not feel tired any more after his sleep in the shade so he put his hats in the barrow again and went on to the market.

NB. The concept of imitation carried by this story.

Staging-posts

1. Man making hats – a number ready to sell
2. Puts hats in barrow
3. Sets out to market
4. Hatmaker tired – hot – rests under branches
5. Falls asleep
6. Monkeys in tree look down – very interested in hats
7. Monkeys come down
8. Each takes hat – puts it on – goes back up tree

9. Man wakes up
10. Sees empty barrow
11. Looks all round – finally up – sees monkeys with hats
12. Shakes fist
13. Monkeys copy
14. Hatmaker has idea
15. Throws hat on ground
16. Monkeys copy
17. Man retrieves hats
18. Continues to market

The Hat Song

(Tune of 'Keel Row')

A red hat, a blue hat
A green hat, a yellow hat
A white hat, a black hat
My hat is on my head

Now change to *shoe* and *sock*, ending with: My shoe/sock is on my foot. Then use other garments and other parts of the body.

References

Garvie, E. (1989) *Story as Vehicle*. Clevedon: Multilingual Matters.

3 The Assessment of Bilingual Children

ANN ROBSON

This paper is based on a set of working papers published by the Department of Psychology, University College London, following a workshop for educational psychologists held in 1989 entitled 'Curriculum Related Assessment with Bilingual Pupils'. As an extension of this work, the paper seeks to present Cummins' theoretical framework of cognitive complexity and contextual demand, and consider its practical application to current National Assessment, including SATs, Standard Tests and Teacher Assessment.

Teachers today are faced with an array of assessments to undertake in the classroom, required either by the school, the local authority or under statutory arrangements. While quality, diversity and accountability were clearly aspirations for education in the 1980s – pursued in part by the establishment of the Standard Assessment Tasks – it now appears that 'a better curriculum, better testing' (Choice and Diversity: A New Framework for Schools (1992): The White Paper) has emerged as a theme for the final decade of the century.

This brings into focus the ethical dilemma for teachers in attempting to provide a 'better curriculum' for bilingual pupils, when this does not sit easily with the proposed 'better testing' arrangements. The work outlined here may help teachers 'test the tests' or, at least the tasks, as well as inform their own routine planning, curriculum delivery and teacher assessment in the classroom.

The text of this paper is in part summarised and adapted from a set of working papers published by the Department of Psychology, University College London, following a workshop in 1989 entitled *Curriculum Related Assessment with Bilingual Children*. A full account of the general approach outlined here and further examples of how the approach may be applied is contained in that publication (Frederickson & Cline, 1990) and grateful acknowledgement is made to the editors and the other educational psychologists who participated in the workshop and wrote the papers from which this text is developed.

The basic issues to consider in the assessment of bilingual pupils are given in the Appendix, and allied to these are several key statements about expectations and views of bilingual pupils underpinning this work. These include:

(a) The view that bilingual children should be considered an advantage in the classroom rather than a problem.
(b) The view that all pupils, including bilingual pupils, should have access to the same Attainment Targets and Programmes of Study as their monolingual peers.
(c) The view that support for bilingual pupils is most fruitfully delivered in the mainstream classroom. On balance bilingual children are found to make most progress where the programme to provide help with their English is designed to support the mainstream curriculum, but with the oral component heightened.
(d) Pupils having difficulty with English because it is their second language should not be equated with pupils with other special educational needs.
(e) Such pupils should not be offered materials with a reduced cognitive demand. From *English for Ages 5-11* (DES, 1988), Chapter 12.

Helping Pupils where Progress Causes Concern

My interest in provision for bilingual pupils and their assessment leads to consideration of that small group of pupils for whom learning appears to teachers as unsuccessful and difficult, or those who simply appear to be failing to make the progress anticipated, however ill-defined. Indeed, most teachers can recall working with a particular bilingual pupil whose progress has given cause for concern. How difficult it appears for many of us to disentangle differences in 'learning the language' from 'learning difficulties' or special educational needs. When such pupils are referred to educational psychologists, subsequent work is undermined by an open acknowledgement of the inadequacy of most traditional assessment procedures and the need for more relevant means and methods to develop our understanding of learning processes at work.

Here the work of Cummins (1984) and Kerr & Desforges (1988) is useful in reminding us that when a child performs badly on quite abstract tasks in the classroom, where there is little support from context, it is easy to assume that failure is due to learning difficulties rather than the lack of the appropriate language skills in English. In order to counter perceived 'learning difficulties' teachers may logically try approaches which involve making the work simpler. This may be done either on an *ad hoc* basis or by task analysis within a behavioural framework. This approach appears to have three major flaws.

- Firstly, simplification of tasks into more and more discrete and isolated steps divorces the learning from the meaningful context. This has the effect of making the work actually harder rather than easier to understand.
- Secondly, evidence of successful learning which is based purely on behavioural objectives – what the child actually does, produces or performs – tends to play down affective factors linked with motivation, self-confidence and anxiety. These factors we know are crucially related to successful language learning.
- Thirdly, this approach relies solely on a transmission model of teaching which gives little leeway for utilising children's previous knowledge and experience within the learning programme. It is important to remember that what the child brings to the learning situation is more important than what is briefly imposed on that child.

Given that in the primary school at least, classroom tasks assume an important role in the assessment of Attainment Targets under the National Curriculum, the model Cummins proposes appears to offer us the means to take the traditional behavioural model of task analysis and regard it with new eyes. Such an approach might thus offer a method of classroom-based assessment more finely tuned to the learning potential of bilingual pupils and more sensitive to a range of evidence for successful learning.

The curriculum related assessment framework offered is based on the work of Cummins (1984). It is regarded as relevant for all pupils in the classroom, but appears particularly appropriate for use with that very small minority of bilingual/bicultural pupils who present teaching difficulties rather than manifesting learning difficulties. This framework brings the curriculum (both the National Curriculum and the school's own broader curriculum) and the teacher to a more central role in the assessment process. This accords with the National Assessment proposals and indeed the framework appears to provide a useful tool in helping develop the required skills for teacher assessment in particular.

Such a framework appears to have a number of potential uses;

(1) *It can be used for topic planning.*
This facilitates differentiation of classroom tasks. It also helps to demonstrate learning achieved at a variety of levels.

(2) *It can be used as a classroom observation tool.*
The framework can be used to show how individual pupils learn and what they need in order to consolidate and extend their experience. It thus offers one way of collecting information about an individual pupil within the context of the working classroom.

(3) *It can be used as a means of analysing curriculum content.*
The framework offers a means of analysing the content of the curriculum and match or mismatch with the learning taking place, i.e. whether the learning taking place is the same as that anticipated within the task content and design.

(4) *It can be used as a means of formative assessment.*
Information gained from such a tool can form the basis for discussion and have practical outcomes in helping plan future teaching programmes and tasks.

(5) *It can be used as a means of contributing to summative assessment.*
For example, the framework can be used in recording achievement at the end of teaching and informing the moderation process.

(6) *It can be used to inform the debate over perceived learning difficulties.*
It can be used as a tool to distinguish perceived learning difficulties from the level of second language development.

The focus of this paper is therefore concerned with how to develop a framework for curriculum related assessment with bilingual children which extends our thinking and practice in terms of teaching and assessment. Effectively we are seeking a method of teacher assessment in a formative sense, that will be suitable for the multilingual classroom, utilising the National Curriculum, the school curriculum and the most relevant curriculum for the pupils in that particular school.

Outline of the Cummins Framework

Research into the language development of bilingual pupils has consistently shown a distinction between conversational ('surface') fluency and the language proficiency necessary to make efficient use of a formal learning situation. Cummins coined the terms 'Basic Inter-personal Communicative Skills' (BICS) to describe the former and

'Cognitive Academic Language Proficiency' (CALP) to describe the latter. On the basis of research carried out on immigrant children in Toronto, Cummins suggested that CALP proficiency levels are not usually reached until five to seven years after the child's introduction to the second language classroom *irrespective of the child's age at entry*, yet most children appear to be fluent at the BICS level within two years of entry.

BICS, then, emerge after about two years of 'immersion' in a second language environment, because by then most children will have gained enough command of pronunciation, vocabulary and grammar to explain to others what they wish to convey in ordinary social situations, and will have sufficiently tuned into the paralinguistic features (e.g. tone, intonation, gesture, facial expression, body posture) and situational cues of social conversation to follow the message others are trying to convey. Even if they have not quite followed, it is usually easy, by a single word or gesture, to get the other to explain, rephrase or elaborate the message. BICS, therefore, is concerned with the child's *intentions*.

CALP is much more closely related to the kind of language proficiency necessary to interpret a more complex, academic communication (when listening or reading), making sense of it by relating it to previous knowledge and experiences, and then creating 'new' knowledge (or rejecting it). It therefore not only involves the surface features of the language, but also complex semantic and functional *meaning*.

The Cummins model

The BICS and CALP model of bilingual language development implies that for a number of years bilingual children will be struggling to make sense of second language classroom instructions and discussion, even if their social language appears to be fluent. This leads to a temptation to make classroom tasks less demanding rather than to explore how they can be made more accessible by modelling, using everyday objects or other contextual cues. To explain the dimensions of language performance more clearly, Cummins developed a model based on both contextual and cognitive dimensions as a theoretical framework with which to analyse the language performance of the child, and indeed, any linguistic activity in the classroom. (See Figure 3.1)

In this model, the horizontal axis represents the continuum relating to the range of contextual support available to children to enable them to express and/or understand meaning. At the 'context embedded' end of the continuum the language is supported by a wealth of situational and paralinguistic cues (pictures, objects, modelling, gesture, etc.) with which

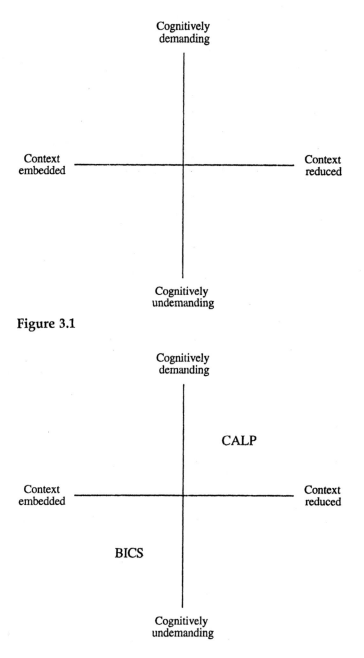

Figure 3.1

Figure 3.2

the children are familiar. At the 'context reduced' extreme, however, children have to be able to interpret meaning exclusively from linguistically subtle and complex communication. Thus, 'story-time' with explicit reference to illustrations of familiar scenes can offer children much contextual support to understanding the verbal message, while listening to a story on tape is much more 'context reduced'.

On the vertical axis, the 'cognitively undemanding' end of the continuum refers to tasks and activities that the child is likely to be familiar with, so that he or she does not need to do much 'thinking' (e.g. talking about your own photographs). At its opposite extreme, 'cognitively demanding' activities are generally unfamiliar and complex, (e.g. talking about others' feelings or possible motivation). By relating Cummins' terms BICS and CALP to the framework of context and cognitive demand, Figure 3.2 could be used as a basic guide for assessment and planning.

Clearly, bilingual pupils are likely to benefit more from the learning experience if their classroom tasks, when 'difficult', are moved across the context embedded continuum rather than down the cognitive dimension. As Cummins (1984: 141) put it: 'The more context embedded the initial L2 input, the more comprehensible it is likely to be, and paradoxically, the more successful in ultimately developing L2 skills in context reduced situations.' (See Kerr & Desforges (1988) for other practical extensions of the model.)

The model's limitations
The Cummins' model is attractively simple as well as versatile. It is however, a *theoretical* framework and– as will be evident from certain applications – has some drawbacks in practice. The most obvious of these is the implication that the cognitive and contextual dimensions are distinct and readily separable. In observing and analysing classroom tasks, instructions and performances, we often find it difficult to disentangle the 'contextual'. In some cases, movement along the contextual dimension has actually been represented on the model as a diagonal shift, as it was found in practice that making tasks or instructions more context embedded also made them somewhat less cognitively demanding. Similarly, changes in cognitive demand may result in tasks actually being presented with greater context embeddedness.

It is also important to remind ourselves of what the framework does not do:

- It does not make allowances for the child's cognitive strategies (e.g.

ability to make inferences) nor the child's learning style (e.g. preference to work independently).
- Before teachers can 'embed' the task, they need to be familiar with the child's cultural background and interests. Clearly, with a culture in transition, it could be self-defeating to rely on stereotypical assumptions.

Thus, ironically, the framework can only be meaningful for the teacher when it, too, is 'context embedded' i.e. when the teacher is clear about the aims of the lesson, knows the child's background well and has tried to match the task to the child's learning style and interest.

How the Model Works in Practice

In looking at how the model works in practice, we need to consider:

(a) What the task requires of the child: an analysis of the task and its cognitive demands.
(b) What the child brings to the task in terms of their experience and current skills.
(c) How the task is presented to the child: to what extent it is context embedded or context reduced.
(d) What is to be acceptable as evidence of learning.
(e) How we assess the quality of different types of evidence of learning.

(a) What the task requires of the child

We first need to consider the 'entry skills' – that is, the skills and knowledge required to enable the child even to attempt the task under consideration, e.g. answering questions about a story requires that the child has established listening skills. The demands of the task itself then have to be considered, particularly the demands on 'Cognitive Academic Language Proficiency'.

(b) What the child brings to the task

In considering whether the child has the experience and skills demanded by the task we need to consider their prior opportunities for play (e.g. with toys, sand and water) and their experience both in their mother tongue and English (e.g. in describing events and objects, in listening to stories, joining in discussion, being familiar with rhymes, songs and accompanying movement).

The child also brings their own expectations and attitudes to a task, whether active or passive, confident or hesitant, solitary or co-operative.

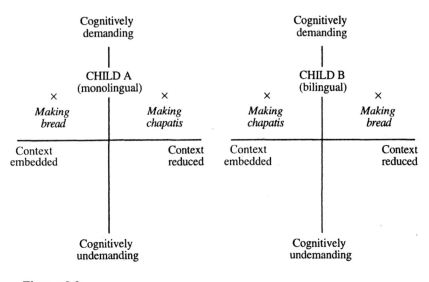

Figure 3.3

We need to consider how much the child shows initiative and willingness to explore and try new solutions. What are the main sources of motivation – does the child wish to please the adults around them; is the child keen to master new tasks? Failure to achieve a task may be related to these factors just as much as to the cognitive ability necessary to meet the task requirement.

In increasing the context embeddedness of a task, and presenting more familiar materials or situations, we not only make the task more relevant to the child, but also enhance their confidence in being able to succeed.

As an example of what different children might bring to a task, consider two children being asked to make bread and chapatis. Child A is a monolingual English speaker whose cultural experiences are European English; child B is a bilingual Panjabi/English speaker whose cultural experiences are Asian English. Assuming (for the sake of argument) that the two tasks – making bread and chapatis – offer similar cognitive demands, we would guess that the context embeddedness is quite different for the two children and that, as a consequence, child A is more likely to be successful in making bread and child B in making chapatis. Moreover, we would expect this to be the case even if neither child had previous direct experience of making bread or chapatis. So the Cummins diagram would be as shown in Figure 3.3.

By observing performance on such a task, we gain information about how the child functions as a learner: what skills and knowledge they bring and what approach they take to the task.

(c) How the task is presented

Tasks may be presented in a variety of ways. Different children will respond more easily and confidently to some tasks than to others: one child may find it easier to respond to information presented in a book, another to a film. As well as the child's familiarity and ease with a particular mode of presentation, there will also be differences in the memory demands imposed -- for example, written instructions can be reviewed, whereas oral ones cannot and must be retained by the listener.

Some of the more common ways of presenting tasks include:

- demonstration of the whole task;
- modelling to the child how to perform the task step by step;
- oral instructions: in English or the mother tongue; (style and complexity of the language used can also vary);
- diagrammatic/pictorial;
- written instructions;
- computer presentation.

An increase in context embeddedness is likely to be achieved by using real objects rather than pictures of objects and by using pictures which depict familiar rather than unfamiliar people. Changes in presentation also affect the cognitive demands – for example, written instructions require that the child is able to read.

As well as differing demands on memory, there are also differences in the opportunities for the child to give feedback on their understanding of what is required and to ask for guidance and help. A teacher working alongside them is well placed to observe how well a child has grasped what is required as well as any potential sources of difficulty; the child following instructions in a workbook has little opportunity for such help and may all too easily persist in making errors or may even not attempt the task at all.

If we consider the example of a bilingual child presented with the task of making a cake but with three different methods of presentation, viz:

- oral instructions given by the teacher in English;
- demonstration of the task by the teacher;
- teacher working alongside the child;

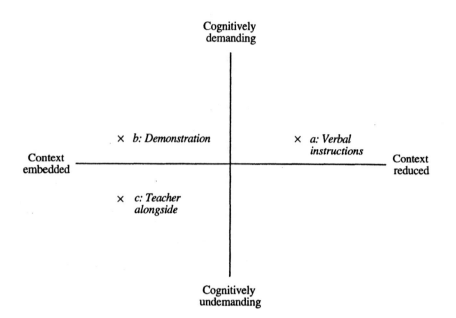

Figure 3.4

then there will be differences in both the cognitive demands and level of context embeddedness as suggested in Figure 3.4.

The above examples tend to consider the child in the setting of a lesson or other adult-directed activity. Yet, in broad terms, a task simply provides the child with the opportunity to respond to the environment.

There is no reason why the Cummins framework should not be used for activities other than those presented by the teacher. For example, observation of the child at play may present evidence of mastery of skills; evidence which is not otherwise easily obtainable.

(d) Evidence of learning

Just as the presentation of a task may vary, so too may the type of responses which are considered as acceptable assessment evidence that a child has mastered a task. The response may be:

- gestural, e.g. pointing;
- action, e.g. building a model;
- drawing;
- oral;

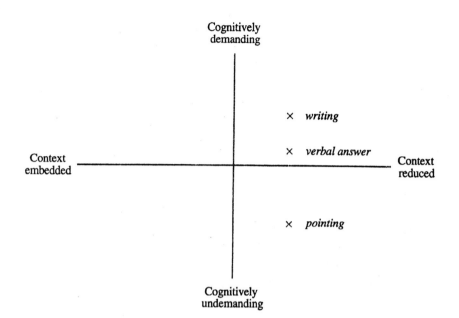

Figure 3.5

- written;
- behaviour in play;
- behaviour reported by parents.

The responses will vary in the cognitive demands they make on the child. For example, writing down an answer is more cognitively demanding than pointing to an object – yet both may give us the required information, e.g. that the child can identify the larger of two objects. Using a more familiar setting, for example, play in the nursery, may enable the child to demonstrate ability to sort objects more readily than they would in a formal test.

The relative difficulty of different ways of responding to the task of selecting the larger of two objects might be represented on the Cummins diagram (Figure 3.5).

In examining the different types of evidence for successful learning we need to be aware of the possibility of other learning which we had not planned! At times this incidental learning can be entirely beneficial, although sometimes the child may not only have failed to learn correctly, but may even have learned something which was incorrect.

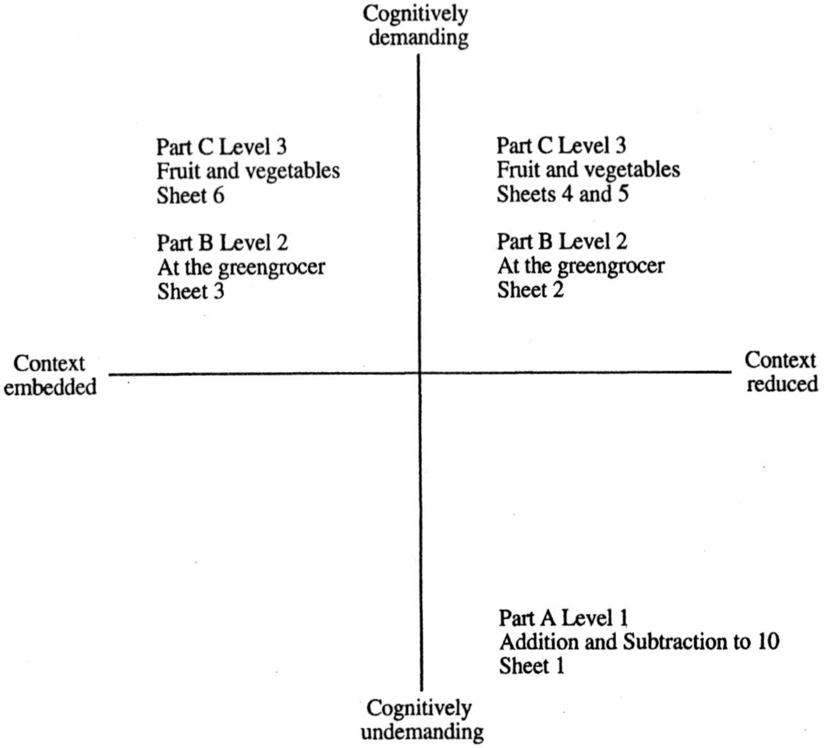

Cognitively
demanding

Part C Level 3
Fruit and vegetables
Sheet 6

Part C Level 3
Fruit and vegetables
Sheets 4 and 5

Part B Level 2
At the greengrocer
Sheet 3

Part B Level 2
At the greengrocer
Sheet 2

Context
embedded

Context
reduced

Part A Level 1
Addition and Subtraction to 10
Sheet 1

Cognitively
undemanding

Figure 3.6 Ma3 Key Stage 1 SAT (1992): analysis for a monolingual indigenous child

(e) The quality of the evidence of learning

Generally we feel more confidence in a child's mastery of a skill if:

- we have observed the child's success ourselves;
- the child can repeat this success;
- it can be extended to a variety of settings and using different materials.

It is important to observe the child in a variety of settings not only to increase the opportunity for them to display mastery, but also to see how firmly established and broadly based the skill is.

In changing the setting it is all too easy to change not only the context embeddedness, but also the cognitive demands of a task, therefore potentially decreasing both the reliability and validity of assessment.

Using the Model in Practice

In order to consider the practical applications of the model in the real-life classroom context, the group of psychologists who originally worked on this project took the framework described here and applied it to work in primary school classrooms in various LEAs. Applications were made and used in observations of children in various contexts including science tasks, making dough, designing pulley-systems, and children involved in mathematical investigations at various levels. The outcomes of these findings are reported in Frederickson & Cline (1990).

We found that the Cummins model was particularly relevant as a tool for formative assessment in that it could offer a framework for ongoing assessment, evaluation of tasks set and the planning of further teaching programmes and tasks for bilingual pupils. Bearing these areas in mind, the model could be seen to have further practical implications for teachers of bilingual pupils in terms of:

(1) Language proficiency, task planning and assessment.
(2) Teaching across the curriculum.
(3) Planning teaching relevant to the Programmes of Study in the National Curriculum.

Applications to Standard Assessment Tasks within National Assessment

Taking this work further, what applications does such a model have when evaluating current national tests, SATs or 'Standard Tasks'? Could such a model be useful not only in improving the quality of teacher assessment, but also in analysing the cognitive and contextual demands of the Standard Tasks themselves? If so, it would therefore inform selection or modification of Standard Tasks where appropriate for particular bilingual pupils.

For example, the 1992 Key Stage 1 SAT for Mathematics (Ma3), might be plotted as shown in Figure 3.6 in thinking of application for a monolingual indigenous child.

Two points relevant to this analysis emerge here. First, let us consider Pupil Sheet 1 (Figure 3.7) which presents a basic computation task using addition.

2+3=5
4+4=
5+1=
7+2=
3+5=
6+4=

Figure 3.7 Ma3 Key Stage 1 SAT (1992): Pupil Sheet 1

While this task may present a context reduced, cognitively demanding task for a low achieving indigenous, English-speaking child, it may well be cognitively undemanding for a bilingual child well-versed in formal mathematics teaching from previous school experience outside the UK. The relative demands of this task could therefore be plotted as shown in Figure 3.8.

Second, what is likely to be more cognitively demanding for the bilingual child is following the oral instruction for recording answers as the child is instructed to write the appropriate number from a mental

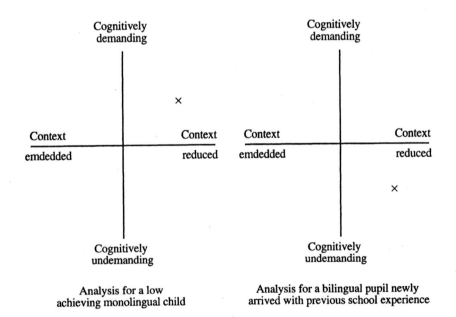

Figure 3.8 Relative task demands represented in Ma3 Key Stage 1 SAT (1992): Pupil Sheet 1

arithmetic sum at speed onto the picture of a pineapple, strawberry or pear – fruit which may be totally unfamiliar and unknown.

On the other hand, we see from analysis of this Standard Assessment Task that Pupil Sheet 6 for Ma3 – an example given of a shopping list – proves by far the most relevant task for work in context. Hence what is presented as the most cognitively demanding task in terms of National Curriculum assessment at this level, is in fact presented in the most appropriate format for bilingual learners, taking into account the Cummins framework relating context and cognitive demand. Those designing Standard Tasks in the future may well need to note such observations, and the value of this type of analysis.

In short the model may act as a useful indicator to alert teachers to the range of cognitive complexity in contextual demands presented in Standard Tasks and Tests and also point to approaches for differentiating these where appropriate (e.g. for pupils with Special Educational Needs).

Future work is needed to apply the model to subsequent SATs and Standard Tests at Key Stages 1, 2, 3 and 4.

Summary

With reference to a bilingual pupil who may have learning difficulties, the Cummins model offers a framework for assessing progress over time, taking into account context, cognitive demand and language ability in relation to the tasks set. It aids planning of teaching and learning relevant to the Programmes of Study at any Key Stage. It helps focus teachers' attention on:

- the task itself;
- the presentation of tasks (e.g. context – including teachers' language);
- the pupil's response to the task.

It helps to focus attention on the possible mismatch between task presentation, the language acquisition of the pupil and task response, and therefore aids the teacher modifying tasks appropriately. With an emphasis on record-keeping in the National Curriculum, the use of this framework for assessment and programme planning provides a useful guide to task planning and progress, and can, therefore, act as one form of record-keeping in itself. The framework is also valuable as a talking point for discussion when planning alternative tasks or cross-curriculum activities within the National Curriculum. In specific cases it can be used to analyse and possibly modify the Standard Assessment Tasks presented currently at Key Stage 1, and in the future for Key Stages 2 and 3.

Finally, Ormark & Watson (1983: 48) call for reconceptualisation of practice which might include, rather than exclude, what the bilingual pupil might bring to assessment situations. It is hoped that the framework presented in this paper may be one such attempt to facilitate the necessary reconceptualisation. The following extract is included as an appropriate conclusion to the paper.

> Any assessment procedure should recognise that culture is not a single entity that every child acquires equally, because each child is unique and confronts the environment in unique ways. The child brings past experiences to the learning situation, as well as individual ways of interacting with the world. The school adds new sets of experiences, but these experiences are uniquely assimilated by each child. The acquisition of knowledge, or cognitive development, is a phenomenon that occurs throughout the years and is not limited to the classroom.
>
> When this broader, interactive, holistic view is taken, there are two ramifications. At the individual assessment level, the assessment process has to reflect as closely as possible the actual experience of each child. For the bilingual exceptional child the major question is not 'How does this child compare with national norms?', but rather 'How does this child compare with the local bilingual population?' At the broader level, research investigations can move beyond asking, 'Did this program help this group versus the control group?' to 'Why did this group succeed or fail?' in terms of the life styles and learning experience with the children involved. One must keep in mind that it is what the child brings to the situation that is more important than what is briefly imposed upon that child.

Appendix: Important Issues to Consider in the Assessment of Bilingual Pupils

(1) Recent research suggests that although it may take up to two years to acquire the skills to be fluent in face-to-face oral communications, it may take between five and seven years to acquire the full range of skills needed to cope with literacy and language in context-reduced situations. (Cummins, 1984)

(2) Some pupils need a considerable length of time before they feel confident enough to join in school activities and use the English they have learned. The need for a silent period is natural and should not

be construed as the child having learning difficulties in the first instance. (Ervin-Tripp, 1979; Hakuta, 1974, in Dulay, Burt & Krashen, 1982)

(3) There are many developmental factors that appear to be common to both native speakers and second language learners in their language development. The pattern of acquisition is not the same for each individual pupil, but broadly speaking both groups of pupils learn in a similar pattern, regardless of their first language background. (Dulay, Burt & Krashen, 1982)

(4) If a pupil appears to be fluent in the daily social routines of the classroom (which are often cognitively undemanding and context embedded), it is easy to assume a similar level of language skills across the board. When the pupil underachieves on more difficult or abstract skills where there is less support from the context, it is easy to assume that failure is due to learning difficulties rather than lack of appropriate language skills. This may not necessarily be correct. (Desforges & Kerr, 1984)

(5) Recent initiatives propose that issues such as monitoring and assessment be built into the school development plan so that information necessary for school-based assessment procedures is automatically part of the working of the school. Teachers who are receiving a child should have some basic information available to them which can be used as a basis on which to plan the work of classes, groups and individuals. (ILEA, 1985)

(6) The distinction should be drawn between special needs (relating to language, culture, overt racism and socio-economic disadvantage) as defined in relation to provision by Section 11 funding, and special educational needs as defined by Warnock and ensuing legislation. (ILEA, 1985)

(7) In the school based assessment procedure we should examine critically whether:
   (a) the curriculum and instruction offered to the pupil is compatible with our knowledge of the way people acquire language and other cognitive skills;
   (b) the school views positively the pupil's cultural heritage and values the contribution this makes to the pupil's education in general;
   (c) Learning which is successful has been set beside that which gives cause for concern. (Robson, 1984)

(8) We often focus on the progress made by bilingual pupils and their developing competence in English. However, the 'mother tongue

skills of bilingual children should be seen as a valuable potential channel for supporting their learning'. A teacher's knowledge of the development and competence in the first language is an important feature of their understanding of a pupil's needs. (ILEA, 1983)

(9) There is now a considerable amount of research to indicate that not only can well-developed conceptual skills in the first language provide a strong foundation for the development of English academic skills, but that bilingualism can be educationally enriching and have a positive effect on intellectual performance. (Cummins, 1984 and Dulay, Burt & Krashen, 1982)

(10) Teachers and other professionals involved in school-based assessment who also speak the languages of the pupils and parents have unique contributions to make in understanding why an individual pupil might be experiencing difficulties. This is not to ignore, however, the perils in the debate with regard to the use of interpreters. What should be pointed out is that discovering more about a pupil's prior learning experiences is extremely important in developing insight into their present functioning. Discussion with parents and other adults from a pupil's social as well as educational community can play a major role in this regard. (Cole in Cummins, 1984)

Adapted from: Robson, A.J. (1987) Bilingual learners: School based assessment. *Gnosis* 10, 33–36. Re-issued through The Questions Publishing Company Ltd.; Birmingham.

References

Cline, T. and Frederickson, N. (1991) *Bilingual Pupils and the National Curriculum: Overcoming Difficulties in Teaching and Learning.* London: University College London.

Cummins, J. (1984) *Bilingualism and Special Education: Issues in Assessment and Pedagogy.* Clevedon: Multilingual Matters.

Department of Education and Science and the Welsh Office (1988) *English for Ages 5–11* (The Cox Report). London: HMSO.

Department for Education (1992) *Choice and Diversity: A New Framework for Schools.* London: HMSO.

Desforges, M. (1982) The assessment of bilingual, bicultural children. *Association of Educational Psychologists Journal* 5 (10), 7–11.

Deforges, M. and Kerr, T. (1984) Developing bilingual children's English in school. *Educational and Child Psychology* 1 (1), 68–80.

Dulay, H., Burt, M. and Krashen, S. (1982) *Language Two.* Oxford: Oxford University Press.

Frederickson, N. and Cline, T. (1990) *Curriculum Related Assessment with Bilingual Children: A Set of Working Papers.* London: University College London.

Inner London Education Authority (1983) *Race, Sex and Class, 2: Multi-Ethnic*

Foundation Education in Schools. London: ILEA.

—(1985) *Educational Opportunities for All?* London: ILEA

Kerr, T. and Desforges, M. (1988) Developing bilingual children's English in school. In G.K. Verma and P. Pumfrey (eds) *Educational Attainments: Issues and Outcomes in Multicultural Education.* London: The Falmer Press.

Ormark, D.K. and Watson, D.L. (1983) Psychological testing and bilingual education: The need for reconceptualisation. In D.R. Ormark and J.G. Erickson (eds) *The Bilingual Exceptional Child.* San Diego: College-Hill Press.

Robson, A. (1984) *Bilingual Learners: Establishing Factors for School Based Assessment.* London: The Unified Language Service, ILEA.

—(1987) Bilingual learners: School based assessment. *Gnosis* 10, 33–6. Reissued through The Questions Publishing Company Ltd.; Birmingham.

4 Towards Equality in the Classroom

FARZANA TURNER and OLA FRANCOMBE

Towards Equality in the Classroom is a series of practical workshops designed to maximise the success of support teachers by encouraging effective relationships with mainstream teachers. Context cards, games, drama and discussion are used by participants to explore and analyse their attitudes and to evolve strategies relevant to their own professional needs.

Race Relations Strategy in Northamptonshire

Northamptonshire County Council is an Authority aware of and concerned about a whole range of issues related to equality of gender and race. Their Race Relations Strategy document, published in April 1989, offers a range of practical strategies to bring about equality of opportunity and promote good relations between persons of different racial groups. It identifies and aims to eliminate unlawful discrimination.

The strategy document has identified seven of the most important issues affecting black and other ethnic minorities in Northamptonshire and has developed a precise procedure for these issues to be brought onto the agendas of a number of County Council departments. One of these is Education. The document states that:

> the explicit objective of the County Council is to make every conscious effort to increase the esteem and understanding of all pupils, students, teachers and lecturers for one another in order to dispel racial prejudice and discrimination. Racism has no place in the Authority's educational institutions and the curriculum will be designed at every stage to promote harmony between those of different races, cultures and creeds.

The County Council will provide training for staff to increase their knowledge of local cultures; of race relations policies and legislation; and to develop their capacity to recognise and combat individual and institutional racism.

The County Council will act to promote equality of opportunity as an employer and in the community through the provision of appropriate education and training.

To this end the following actions are identified as part of the strategy:

- Develop a curriculum to reflect the educational needs of children from a multicultural society. Meeting the specific linguistic needs of children who speak English as a second language (ESL).
- Training to be given to school headteachers about the extent to which racist attitudes and practices can influence teacher expectations relative to ethnic minority children.
- School headteachers to be encouraged to take action where necessary to ensure that the ethos of classrooms and staff-rooms is not influenced by racist attitudes and practices.
- Practical measures to eradicate racial bias (individually and institutionally) through anti-racist training; INSET courses; seminars; and consultative meetings between ethnic minority parents, teachers, governors, community organisations and local authority officers.
- School governors to be informed and trained as to how racism can and does affect ethnic minority children's school performance.
- Each school to carry out a critical review of its allocation procedures to ensure that a child's ability (irrespective of their colour) is the sole criterion upon which they will be placed into any teaching group.
- The monitoring of GCSE and other examination results to show:
  (a) The type and number of subjects taken by children from each ethnic group.
  (b) The number of passes gained and the grades obtained by each child per subject taken.
  (c) The number of ethnic minority children compared with white children who leave school in any year without qualifications.

Use the data gathered to identify underachievement and devise strategies to combat it.

Northamptonshire Multicultural Education Service

The Multicultural Education (MCE) Service is part of the Northamptonshire Inspectorate and Advisory Service (NIAS).

We believe that every school in Northamptonshire should offer a curriculum which is of the highest quality and which prepares children and young people to become full and active citizens in a multiethnic and multicultural society. The curriculum should also challenge stereotypes based on gender, race or ability and provide equal access and educational outcome for all pupils.

The 1988 Education Reform Act reinforces the concept of entitlement and equal opportunities for all. As well as this, legislation within the Race Relations Act supports and regulates what is expected in terms of equitable and just treatment.

Members of the MCE Service work with pupils, schools and other education establishments, parents and counties to:

- ensure equality of opportunity in all respects of the educational process;
- work towards equality of outcome for all pupils;
- enable schools and other authorities to meet their statutory responsibilities in relation to legislation on race, sex and ability.

The Multicultural Education Service in Northamptonshire is headed by the General Inspector for Multicultural Education. The Senior Management Team consists of four Advisory Teachers/Project Leaders who lead specific teams which provide support and advice to schools, institutions, communities and organisations across the county in the following areas:

- Equal Opportunities.
- Achievement of African-Carribean pupils.
- Achievement of Bangladeshi pupils.
- English as a Second Language.
- Home/School Liaison.
- Traveller Education.
- Community Languages and Mother Tongue Teaching.

Teams also have other senior staff who assist in the overall co-ordination of services offered and, with the Inspector and Advisory Teachers, form the management team for the whole Multicultural Education Service.

Teachers/Officers working for the Service are assigned to specific schools, institutions or organisations on a long-term or peripatetic basis. Day-to-day management of staff is therefore shared between the senior managements of the Service and of the schools and institutions in which staff are placed.

Alongside the work in mainstream schools, the Service is also involved in supporting the development of Supplementary Schools, organised and run by local minority ethnic groups to maintain their linguistic and cultural heritage.

In 1992, major revisions were made to Section 11 funding arrangements. All provision from April 1992 was to be made under time limited 'projects'. In the schools' sector Northamptonshire applied for and was successful in having four projects approved.

Each project focuses on meeting specific needs, identified by schools and communities. The projects are intended to enable full participation by pupils and their families in all aspects of education in Britain. Support is targeted and monitored closely and regular consultation takes place involving senior management in schools and the Service, community organisations, officers of the local authority and elected members. The four projects are as follows:

English as a second language

Many minority ethnic children start school having acquired linguistic skills in their home language but have limited competence in English. As well as this there continue to be older pupils newly arrived in Britain who need to learn English in order to participate within the educational system in this country.

This project is concerned with providing direct teaching support to pupils in all age phases and, as far as possible, at each stage of English language learning. The project is also concerned with giving advice and support to teachers in developing appropriate strategies for working with bilingual pupils.

Pupils in the early years of their schooling are supported by bilingual assistants who speak the children's mother tongue, so that English language learning can be developed through fluency in the child's first language.

Some teachers are attached to one school only, while others visit a number of schools on a peripatetic basis; all teachers within the project aim to work in partnership with mainstream teachers to ensure that English as a Second Language needs are met.

Achievement of African-Carribean and Bangladeshi pupils

The two projects have been established in response to needs identified by schools and within these specific communities. Northamptonshire has undertaken ethnic monitoring of GCSE results over the last three years and these groups have been identified as generally achieving at a lower level than the county average; Key Stage 1 SATs results have also given cause for concern.

The two Achievement Projects are intended to assist schools in addressing this underachievement. Support is provided to identified schools in all phases by a team of school-based and peripatetic teachers. Some school-based teachers are also involved in the ESL Project. All posts are based in either Northampton or Wellingborough.

Home/School Liaison

It has long been accepted that the involvement of parents/carers is a desirable, if not essential, element in the educational process, yet some parents, including many from ethnic minority groups, do not participate fully in this process for a variety of reasons.

Teachers from the Multicultural Education Service have always aimed to make links with the homes of pupils, and through this project it is possible to extend these links.

Home/School Liaison Officers are not necessarily trained teachers but they have an understanding of the education system, including the National Curriculum and Assessment. They share the languages and cultural backgrounds of the main ethnic minority communities in Northamptonshire and are thus better able to encourage and facilitate increased parental participation in informal and formal school activities. The officers also support and encourage members of ethnic minority communities in becoming interested in school governorship.

The Home/School Liaison Officers share linguistic and cultural heritage with the following communities: Afro-Carribean; Bengali/Sylheti; Chinese; Gujerati; Panjabi; and Urdu.

Traveller Education Service

Local Education Authorities are able to apply for additional funding from the DES grant for the Education of Traveller and of Displaced Persons. In 1991 Northamptonshire submitted a proposal and had approval for a grant for three years. The grant is intended for additional education provision for Traveller pupils. Support for Traveller pupils in the county is organised into a centralised service.

Under the regulations, 'Travellers' include Gypsy and other Travellers living on either authorised or unauthorised sites, Showmen (Circus/ Fairground) and bargee families. Within Northamptonshire there are a relatively high number of authorised sites, with low turn-over; most unofficial encampments are moved on within days. Three private fairgrounds and two circuses spend the winter in yards within the county.

There are around 200 Traveller pupils attending in excess of 20 Northamptonshire schools; support staff work within a geographical cluster of schools to enable smooth cross-phase transfer and closer links with Traveller Communities based in different areas. As Showman families often move weekly between Easter and October, the support teacher with this specific responsibility works closely with the 'Winter' schools developing distance learning programmes. These are monitored through contact with pupils and their families and supplemented with summer visits by a network of support teachers throughout the country.

A Practical Approach to the Classroom Situation

The programme presented on the course in York relates to a number of areas of action specified in the Strategy Document. Our Service has been looking at ways of maximising the effectiveness of support teachers. We have identified as particularly significant the development of successful working partnerships with mainstream teachers and the locking of these into the context of appropriate and effective whole school policies.

We feel that we must resist pressure to be targeting too narrowly the ethnic minority children with whom we work; in some way the class as a whole must be involved. Balancing these factors is a crucial challenge which we try in our programme to elucidate and explore.

It is necessary that the role of the support teacher should be understood and valued in the school in order to realise its fullest potential and to avoid being marginalised or looked upon as merely the visitor who pops in to help little Sanjit and Nisha.

Towards Equality in the Classroom is an INSET programme which was originally devised by senior members of Northamptonshire MCE Service for teachers working with bilingual pupils and Travellers' children, but has proved equally valuable to other support teachers working in a mainstream situation. By means of a series of practical workshops, it investigates the relationship between support and mainstream teachers, and by examining both points of view explores the most effective ways to maximise mutual success.

The programme consists of:

- General introduction – 'A personal view'.
- 'Cards on the table' – an investigation of one's own perceptions and attitudes, both overt and unrecognised. This is done in small groups by using the device of a card game which is designed to increase level of self-awareness in a non-threatening way. Cards are coded in such a way as to explore and analyse perceptions of 'role' and working practice.
- 'The other side of the coin' – a mildly satirical presentation of a not unfamiliar staffroom drama designed to provoke comment and discussion. The aim is to examine the concerns of support and mainstream teachers about each other's roles. These concerns include the responsibilities, benefits and challenges of working together. In our experience, this part of the programme stimulates profitable discussion of partnership teaching and effective strategies for establishing the credibility of support teachers within schools. It highlights the paramount importance of liaison and communication between support and mainstream staff.

  This part of the programme concludes with a group of quotes from case studies, in each of which viewpoints of the class teacher, the support teacher and the child are presented.

- 'Putting things in context' – this is a workshop using context cards relating to the work of support teachers. It is structured for small groups. Participants are reassured at the outset that there is no 'correct' response. It is anticipated that discussion will reflect the various pressures and tensions within each context rather than finding the 'right' answer.
- 'Facing up to reality' – a plenary session which is developed out of the products of the workshops. Some of the results are surprising – participants report valuable insights and practical solutions to identified challenges.

The programme lasts two and a half hours. All the above details were accurate at the time of presentation. For current information please contact Ola Francombe or Chris Derrington at Wellingborough Professional Development Centre, 86 Stanley Road, Wellingborough, Northants. NN8 1DY. Telephone Wellingborough (01933) 272462. Our team of trainers can be available to run INSET courses based on this programme.

5 Towards Bilingualism in the Primary School: Supporting New Arrivals as they Acquire English – a Scottish Perspective

ANN HINDLE

Towards Bilingualism in the Primary School is a videopack designed to offer initial support to primary schools in non-urban and some urban situations which may have little or no experience of welcoming bilingual pupils. It is seen as a useful resource for whole school staff development. This paper details the development of the pack and introduces the main components.

As an introduction I will give a description of the area in which I work. I am based in the city of Edinburgh, with the more rural areas of East Lothian, Midlothian and West Lothian surrounding us. These three areas plus the city make up Lothian Region.

Our bilingual communities include the more settled groups who speak Cantonese, Panjabi, Urdu and Bengali. We also have short stay business and student groups who speak mainly Arabic or Japanese. In 1990/91 we worked with pupils who spoke more than 40 different languages.

It is worth mentioning that the Scottish education system differs from that of England and Wales in the following ways:

(1) We have no National Curriculum – but we do have 5–14 National Guidelines.
(2) We have no SATs – this term is not used in Scotland. National Testing at P4 (age 8–9) and P7 (age 11–12) has just begun.
(3) There is no Section 11 funding. A centre-based peripatetic service is

more the norm. Bilingual pupils are supported within mainstream schools, additional support being given to the school by an ESL visiting teacher. Most ESL teachers have the RSA Diploma in Teaching English across the Curriculum in Multilingual Schools.

(4) Primary classes are a maximum of 33, or 25 if composite classes.

I hope this brief introduction has set the scene. My focus is *not* on the few city-centre primary schools who have a continuous ESL teacher presence, who have a constant flow of bilingual pupils, and who have developed a great amount of awareness and expertise. These schools account for about 20 or so in Central Edinburgh and 50 or so in Central Glasgow, but my focus in this paper is on the *hundreds* of other primary schools throughout Scotland in non-urban situations who have little or no experience of welcoming bilingual pupils and who are faced from time to time with this new challenge!

A frequent scenario for myself in Edinburgh is a telephone call from a school in Lothian Region or elsewhere. I receive calls from Shetland to Dumfries asking for advice and guidance, having just enrolled a new pupil. Lothian schools demand instant resources, which are not available. A conversation may begin:

'We have just enrolled/are about to enrol some pupils who don't speak English.'

I may ask:

'What language do they speak?'

Often the reply is:

'I don't know.'

Or:

'Indian'.

Other comments may be:

'She hasn't been to school yet and she is six.'

And:

'Do you come and teach them English?'

So starts a slow but necessary process advising schools on:

- initial placement;
- visiting the school, arranging meetings with the head teacher, the family, and an interpreter if needed;
- talking to the class teachers.

This can be a slow time-consuming but necessary process which is frequently repeated. Perhaps a one-off in-service session with the staff is arranged. Always there is a genuine wish to do what is best but often there is little knowledge or awareness. This may be a familiar scenario to others.

So this was the starting place for our project *Towards Bilingualism in the Primary School*. I worked with John Landon, Senior Lecturer in Multicultural Education at Moray House Institute of Education, Heriot-Watt University. Our aim was to provide a self-access pack which head teachers could borrow for whole school staff development, so that schools may be better prepared and aware of the needs of their bilingual pupils.

Our three general aims were:

(1) To support school staff over initial fears and worries – to reassure.
(2) To create awareness of the *needs* of bilingual pupils.
(3) To show the valuable asset of a bilingual teacher and the role of the class teacher.

We outline the importance of:

(1) A welcoming school ethos – role of staff, school notices, families' first impressions.
(2) Awareness of pupil's previous experience and background, both educational and cultural, and to provide pupils with opportunities to demonstrate previous learning.
(3) Involving pupils in mainstream activities from the start.
(4) The vital role of the peer group.
(5) How the ESL support teacher can work with the mainstream teacher, but that there is a lot the class teacher can do without the ESL support when it is not available.

The pack consists of a video and a booklet for three workshop sessions, each lasting approximately one and a half hours. The workshops are written so that a headteacher with little personal experience of bilingual pupils could lead three one and a half hour sessions with the school staff.

The video was made in the new town of Livingston where two families arrived (four new pupils), early in the new school year. One family had come from Bradford and the other from Pakistan. We focused on two pupils: one girl of P3 age (7–8) who had had no previous formal schooling, and her older brother of 12 (P7 age) who was fluent and literate in his home language.

The video is used as an introduction to the workshops. Participants in York had the opportunity to try out three tasks from the seven included.

The workshops are:

(1) Creating an Appropriate Learning Environment.
(2) Enrolment and Preliminary Assessment.
(3) Providing Appropriate Support in the Mainstream Classroom.

This videopack is now available for purchase, priced £18. The price includes permission for unlimited photocopying within the purchasing establishment. A substantial discount is available to Authorities who prefer to purchase centrally on behalf of their teaching establishments. The packs are available from: Mrs Wendy Laird, Publications Unit, Westwood House, 498 Gorgie Road, Edinburgh, EH11 3AF.

As a result of feedback from the group in York, some changes were made to the statements used in Task One. The final discussion proved stimulating and informative and contributed to the final version of the videopack.

Supporting New Arrivals as they Acquire English: Creating an Appropriate Learning Environment – Video (allow 20 minutes)

Workshop 1, Task One (approximately 40 minutes)

In this workshop we concentrate on statements which have been selected to represent approaches to creating an appropriate learning environment for new arrivals who use a language other than English at home.

- Form small groups of four or five.
- You have 16 statements (see Figure 5.2), and you are asked to select from these the *nine* which seem particularly apt in creating an appropriate learning environment for the 'new arrival'. This means, of course, that you must discard seven cards.
- With the remaining nine, through discussion, decide on an agreed order of importance. BE SURE TO ASK OTHER GROUP MEMBERS TO CLARIFY WHAT THEY UNDERSTAND EACH STATEMENT TO MEAN. (It may well be different from the meaning you would give it.)
- In ordering your nine cards place them in the diamond shape in Figure 5.1.

In creating an appropriate school and class environment for the 'new arrival', which nine of the statements in Figure 5.2 must we pay attention to?

Most Important

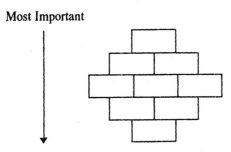

Least Important

Figure 5.1

Workshop 3, Task Two: Providing appropriate support in the main-stream classroom

Work in groups of three.

(a) Two members of each group should work out the meaning and requirements of the task <Condutores de carros – a written comprehension in Portuguese>, while the third member observes and notes down the strategies which they use, and the degree to which they employ knowledge and skills which they already possess. PLEASE DO NOT CONSULT THE ENGLISH TRANSLATION.

(b) Together, the three decide on the kind of support they would have found useful to make the task fully accessible to them, as learners, whilst drawing on the skills and knowledge which they already possess. A rough translation of the passage is provided to assist you with this.

Task Three: Support Strategies

Work in three groups.

Watch the video of work in the classroom again, and look for examples of support in terms of the categories suggested in Figure 5.3. Collate your findings, and you will have guidelines on initial support for new arrivals for whom English is a second language.

1. We should know which language(s) the family is using at home.	9. All staff, teaching and non-teaching, should be sensitive to, and provide for, the different cultural backgrounds of families within the school.
2. Since the child is learning English in school, we should encourage parents to use English at home.	10. It's important for the child to learn to fit in with our ways as quickly as possible.
3. The range of Resources and Curriculum content in school should reflect the multicultural nature of British society.	11. We should discover which skills and concepts have already been acquired through the mother tongue and seek to help the child's development to continue.
4. The new pupil can work with the slow learners until he/she catches up with the rest of the class.	12. If possible we should provide opportunities for children sharing a common mother tongue to use this language in group activities.
5. We should be aware of the correct spelling and pronunciation of the pupil's name.	13. We should take positive action to create opportunities for their parents to contribute to school life.
6. We should assume that the child really understands more English than he/she can produce.	14. We should treat them the same as all other children, otherwise we will emphasise their differences and *create* a problem.
7. We should encourage the parents to support their children's education by sending home books written in their mother tongue for home reading.	15. We should group children with able speakers of English, when planning classroom activities.
8. We should assume that the child needs help with the very basics when he/she enters our school.	16. If the child won't speak English we should encourage him/her to do so by working in a one to one teacher/ pupil situation.

Figure 5.2

GROUP	SUPPORT CATEGORY	EXAMPLES FROM VIDEO
1	Visual support	
	Peer support	
	Modelling by teacher	
	Stimulus in mother tongue	
	Space for innovation and exploration	
	Appropriateness to age of pupil	

Figure 5.3

6   The Welsh Perspective on Working with Bilingual Children in the Primary School

WILLIAM H. RAYBOULD

This paper gives a detailed account of bilingual children in Welsh primary schools. After an introduction to set the scene, the discussion begins with a description of the position of the Welsh language in general (within Wales). The place of Welsh in the field of education is documented, and then, more specifically, the workings of nursery and primary schools. Comparisons are made with other parts of the world such as Canada where, as in Wales, English-speaking children know that their teachers can understand their mother tongue, even though they may be being taught through the medium of another language (French or Welsh). The contrast between this situation and the position of bilingual children in England is pointed out. The paper ends with a discussion of home languages other than Welsh and English and Section 11 funding in Wales. In effect, the paper is an edited transcript of the actual presentation given in York in March 1992. This unusual format was chosen to reflect the importance of the input from the floor.

Introduction

The theme of the In-Service Course, 'Working with Bilingual Children', was how conscious of the conventions of language use we become when speakers of many languages come together to share ideas, and, in particular, ideas about how languages are learned. Bilingual people tend to have an awareness often lacking in monolingual people of the distinction between languages which we want to use, *preferred* languages, and languages which we need to use, *target* second languages.

In Britain, formal education is compulsory for all children, and in the education provided by the state, it is the normal expectation that this will be through the medium of English. A child whose mother tongue is English can be confident that their teacher will understand what they say or write. In Wales, a child who is bilingual in Welsh and English, but whose preferred language is Welsh, has the right to use the mother tongue protected by the Orders for the National Curriculum, if they attend a Welsh-medium school. This is because, as a result of the lengthy struggle for institutional recognition of the right to speak Welsh in Wales, primary school teachers are trained and carry out their duties in a culture of positive interactive bilingualism.

This is not necessarily the case in England, where the result of the identification of proficiency in language with proficiency in English is that the language which the bilingual child wants to use may not be the language they need to use. Furthermore, in Wales, the child whose mother tongue is English but who is being taught through the medium of Welsh, has the knowledge and confidence that they are understood by their teachers while they are being instructed in the new language, even before they can fully understand what is being said in the classroom. Children who have other non-Welsh mother tongues, such as Arabic, Bengali, Chinese, French, German, Hindi, Italian, Japanese, Polish, Panjabi, Sylheti, Urdu or Vietnamese, benefit from the same opportunity to learn Welsh as a Second Language, systematically, as a language of instruction and personal communication, if they attend Welsh-medium schools.

They are likely to be less sure of being understood by their teachers when they speak their mother tongue than English-speaking children would be, but when they are being instructed in Welsh as a Second Language they are not measured in their language proficiency against norms established for native speakers. Their learning of Welsh will be supported, enabled and assessed by realistic standards in Welsh-medium schools. In Welsh-speaking areas, their learning of Welsh, however, will be as essentially 'sink or swim' as their learning of English.

'The National Curriculum and Bilingual Children in England' is significantly different from 'The National Curriculum and Bilingual Children in Wales', because Wales is a bilingual country. In England, 'bilingual' is understood to mean 'speaking English and one or more other languages'; in Wales, 'bilingual' is generally taken to mean 'speaking English and Welsh'; children who would be referred to in England as 'bilingual' would be 'trilingual' in Wales. An unthinking emphasis on monolingualism as 'normal' compromises the sense of 'normality' in the language use of the bilingual child. As Cummins (1979) has pointed out, children whose school experience does not yield them a sense of self-worth, of validated identity, may be hampered in their cognitive development, not merely their linguistic proficiency. A child in primary school frequently expects to not understand (that is what school is for – to teach you what you do not know), but a child is very threatened by the experience of not being understood by those who have that child in their care. This point is very clearly made by the Children Act 1989.

Discussion

WR = William Raybould

WR: One of the best things to do is to start with this document, which is *Statistics of Education in Wales, Ystadegau Addysg yng Nghymru*. It's a bilingual document, on the front anyway, but inside it's monolingual, in English, and there's no reference in it to teaching bilingual children, certainly not as you would understand bilingual children. What they *do* have in this document is a whole section on Welsh, as a subject and as a medium. So, there is apparently no reason for the Welsh Office to consider the funding of and the assessment of bilingual children as such, and that area which *you* are mostly concerned with in your professional work has disappeared from the Welsh Office's view of education. The corresponding document for England would have a whole section on working with bilingual children, 'ethnic minorities' or 'community languages'. And I think that you should understand why that is so.

This is *The Other Languages of England* and obviously, as soon as I picked up the document in the library, I looked for the word 'Welsh'. And the actual index says: 'Welsh: majority language, page 110'. That shocked me. I don't consider Welsh to be a majority language… what I have to say today may explain why that is the view of the Welsh language that the Welsh Office hold, which I think that the DES in London have as well. Welsh as a majority language is something I look forward to.

FROM THE FLOOR (FLF):   Not even in Wales?

WR: No.

FLF: Only in certain parts.

WR: No, never in this century. I'd like to show you some of the details of why that is so. So let's go through some diagrams.

See Figure 6.1 for where you locate Wales on the map of Great Britain – it's a very interesting sociological comment on where Wales

Figure 6.1 Broad economic regional divisions of UK

is. I did study History, and a little bit of Archaeology in College, and in those days they had a line across Britain, which was Lowland Zone and Highland Zone, Britannia Inferior and Britannia Superior. In York you're in Britannia Inferior. And that's the kind of feeling we have about where Wales is, it's on the periphery, if you like.

[Referring to a book entitled *Darganfod Hanes Cymru, Discovering the History of Wales* (Oxford University Press)]: What we've [that is, the Welsh Joint Education Committee, Cydbwyllgor Addysg Cymru, for whom W.R. works] produced, in conjunction with Oxford University Press over the last five years, is a whole series of books introducing History in the National Curriculum for the children in schools. They were started before the National Curriculum came in, so they aren't totally relevant, but nevertheless I think they are very attractive. And what they have done for the children of Wales is to identify the location of Wales in as attractive a way as possible.

There'd be the typical young children's idea of: I live in Main Street, Any Town, and you end up in the Universe, don't you? So that's the kind of view we've got, and obviously we've made use of the latest technology in as attractive a way as possible, the principle being that although you need a lot of financial support and central government support, we want to provide the children who are working in Wales with materials that are every bit as attractive – and give them the feeling of self-worth that any child working through the medium of English would, in Wales. (And that is an issue for you: how do you produce materials that are going to give the child that feeling of self-worth?)

Table 6.1 Percentage of the population able to speak Welsh 1901–81

County 4 (pre-1974)	1901	1911	1921	1931	1951	1961	1971	1981
Anglesey	91.7	88.7	84.9	87.4	79.8	75.5	65.7	61.0
Brecon	45.9	41.5	37.2	37.3	30.3	28.1	22.9	19.3
Caernarfon	89.6	85.6	75.0	79.2	71.7	68.3	62.0	59.7
Cardigan	93.0	89.6	82.1	87.1	79.5	74.8	67.6	63.2
Carmarthen	90.4	84.9	82.4	82.3	77.3	75.1	66.5	60.0
Denbigh	61.9	56.7	48.4	48.5	38.5	34.8	28.1	24.2
Flint	49.1	42.2	32.7	31.7	21.1	19.0	14.7	13.5
Glamorgan	43.5	38.1	31.6	30.5	20.3	17.2	11.8	10.0
Merioneth	93.7	90.3	82.1	86.1	75.4	75.9	73.5	68.2
Monmouth	13.0	9.6	6.4	6.0	3.5	3.4	2.1	2.7
Montgomery	47.5	44.8	42.3	40.7	35.1	32.3	28.1	24.0
Pembroke	34.4	32.4	30.3	30.6	26.9	24.4	20.7	18.1
Radnor	6.2	5.4	6.3	4.7	4.5	4.5	3.7	5.0
Wales	49.9	43.5	37.1	36.8	28.9	26.0	20.8	18.9

Source: Based on Aitchison & Carter (1985: 8 and 20)

The column that's very important for you to look at in Table 6.1 is 1901, for 49.9%. The 1901 Census was the Census which showed that the population of Wales was at its peak. We've never had as many people living in Wales as there were in 1901, and at that time the population of people who were Welsh-speakers was less than 50%. And the reason for that was that, as one of our prominent historians has said, Wales was very much in a colonial situation. People emigrated to Wales to work, as an alternative to emigrating to Pennsylvania to work. A number of Welsh people emigrated to

Pennsylvania to work in the mines, but there were many more people who emigrated from the rural areas of Wales to the industrial areas of Wales to work. And many more people came from Cornwall, Scotland and Ireland to work in Wales. So Welsh has never been a majority language in the modern era [i.e. in the 20th century].

In 1981 the figure is 18.9%. The Welsh Office are not going to bring out any 1991 population statistics, and certainly not any language statistics, until September in the first instance for one of the counties of Wales, the smallest county, and we won't have the actual corresponding figure for the 1991 Census for perhaps another two or three years. My hope is that it will be over 20%. I'll give you the reasons. Some comments on that kind of issue are in the document *Welsh Language Planning: Opportunities and Constraints*.

That article was an article that I delivered in Galicia last September, and I co-operated with Colin Williams, who is Professor of Geography at Stafford Polytechnic. The issue of the language decline is dealt with in the first chapter or so.

Figure 6.2 tries to show the nature of the movement of the language frontiers: 70% is the point we are trying to identify. If 70% of the population are Welsh-speaking, you can say it's a majority language in that community. And since 1750 [in some parts of Wales] that border has never been further east than effectively where it is now. Look at the centre of Wales, at a place like Newtown, very close to Aberystwyth. That hasn't moved in three centuries. It's effectively at the same point. Where the language *has* moved is along the industrial border, South Wales. The industrial area has moved steadily west... and I'll show you a succession of maps.

Figure 6.3 is in terms of the Welsh-speaking population who read and write Welsh, so these are the people who consider themselves to be Welsh-speaking. In the Census that we had last year, there was a language question, which I am sure you took great interest in. I don't know whether it was comprehensive enough. I don't know whether it actually gave the information you would like the government to have. It certainly wasn't as far as the Welsh were concerned, because they offered the population of Wales a choice of saying:

I speak Welsh.   I read Welsh.   I write Welsh.

And some people said: 'Well, if I don't speak, read and write Welsh, I can't say I speak Welsh'. So they don't reply: 'Yes'. What we need is a

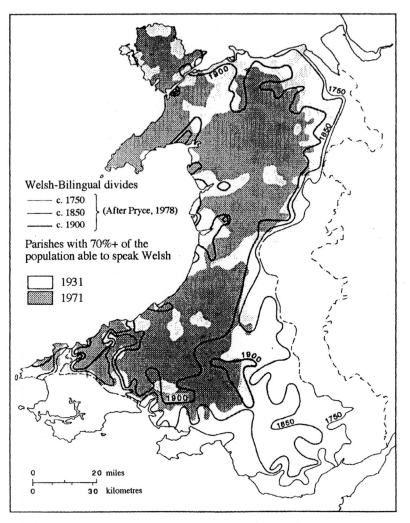

Figure 6.2 Successive language frontiers between 1750 and 1971.
Source: Williams and Raybould (1991: 26)

language audit, which tells us how many speak it well, whether they speak it in the house, whether they speak it in work, whether they speak it in the chapel. But some people say: 'Oh, I speak Welsh with my children but I never speak it at work. I don't speak Welsh'. Because the phrase: 'I speak Welsh' or 'I don't speak Welsh' refers to their habit, not their ability. They could, but they don't, so they don't write: 'I speak Welsh'. So that 18.9% in Table 6.1 is effectively the solid core *minimum*

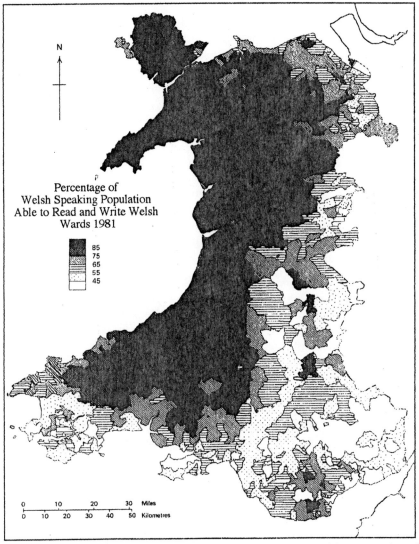

Figure 6.3 Percentage of Welsh-speaking population able to read and write Welsh.
Source: Aitchison & Carter (1985: Map 8)

of Welsh speakers, because everybody else says 'Oh no, my Welsh isn't good enough'. It's the self-image again, and the Census makes people very, very aware of that.

The Secretary of State for Wales has been receiving letters, requests, from people in Wales for the last 50 years to ask the crucial questions in the Census concerning language, and they've not listened to those kinds of request at all, because their purposes are not the purposes of those who are concerned about the development of the Welsh language. From our point of view, there should have been simply a question:

'What do you consider to be your first language?'

And they could have gone on from there to ask any number of questions, which would have actually allowed you, as bilingual people, to say more about your bilingualism. It would have been something that applied to the whole United Kingdom. I don't think Wales is separate from the rest of the United Kingdom in its concern for bilingualism. It's just that the government find that a question which they can't really address financially.

I will now compare Figure 6.4 with Figure 6.3. The dark area on Figure 6.3 is effectively the mountains, everything over a thousand feet. That's where the percentage of the Welsh-speaking population is over 70%. Why? Because you've only got five people living in every square mile, and most of them are Welsh-speaking. That's important to consider. In the North, it's over a thousand feet; in the South, over five hundred feet (a hill). Now that's where the density of Welsh speakers is, according to the percentage on Figure 6.3. Now compare where the Welsh-speaking people live according to Figure 6.4. They don't correspond at all. So Colin Williams, being a geographer, put those two maps (Figure 6.3 and Figure 6.4) together, producing Figure 6.5.

Superimposing one map over the other, he showed the *dislocation* between those areas that are majority Welsh-speaking and those areas that contain most Welsh-speakers. To explain: in the shaded areas on Figure 6.5, 70% of the population speak Welsh, so you can call them 'the Heartland of Wales'. They are the Welsh-speaking areas where you would expect to find the local pub, the local chapel, the local shop, all with Welsh-speakers serving in them. But, the density of population in that area is low, because it's rural and mountainous. There aren't many people there. The large circle in the South East is Cardiff, and there are over 17,000 Welsh-speakers there. If you look at the previous map (Figure 6.4), in a place like Llandewi Brefi, you've got somewhere in the region of perhaps 500 at the most. So, there are 500 there, where 70% of the population are Welsh-speaking, and there are 17,000 in the Cardiff area. So, where the Welsh-speakers are, they're in a minority, and that

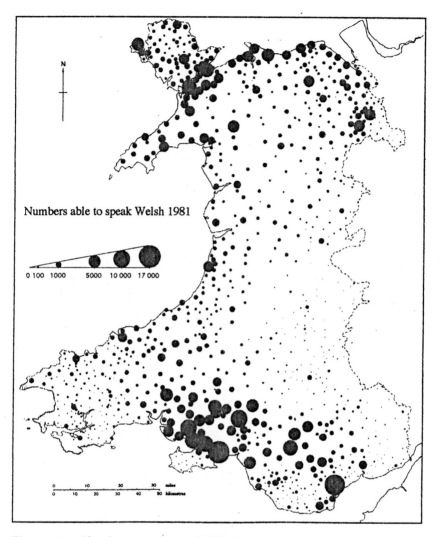

Figure 6.4 Absolute numbers of Welsh speakers in 1981.
Source: Aitchison & Carter (1985: Map 2)

is one of the great difficulties. This is the crucial issue.

The overlap of shaded areas and large dots in South Wales on Figure 6.5 [i.e. Cwm Gwendraeth in Dyfed] is a highly industrialised area of Wales. It's the area where there have been coal-mines until today. They've practically all gone in Wales, but there was still one coal-mine

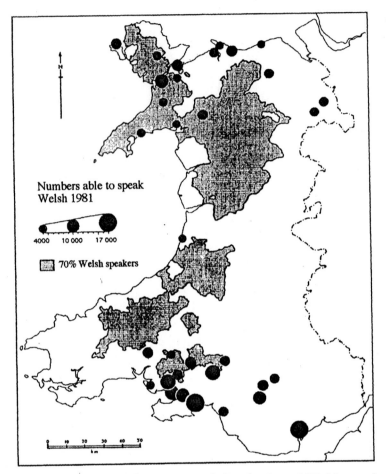

Figure 6.5 Absolute and proportional distribution of Welsh speakers in 1981.
Source: Williams & Raybould (1991: 28)

in this area, which actually closed last week. There was a programme on the radio about the Welsh-speaking miners which I was listening to in the car as I was travelling up to York. They were describing the closure of that mine, which means that there is no longer a mine in Wales which is predominantly Welsh-speaking, where the workers discuss their everyday work in the Welsh language. They are actually making a film of the last years, to make sure they have a recording of the actual miners speaking, in Welsh, about their everyday work and life. It's the last opportunity. That mine is in the middle of the area

1. **Idealism:** *the construction of a vision of a fully rehabilitated 'threatened' language, this is the issue of making language and nation coterminous.*

2. **Protest:** *mobilising sections of the population to agitate for a social reform-revolution in the promotion of the lesser-used language.*

3. **Legitimacy:** *securing a generalised acceptance of the normalcy of exercising language rights in selected domains.*

4. **Institutionalisation:** *ensuring that the language is represented in key strategic agencies of the state, i.e. the law, education, and public administration.*

5. **Parallelism/Normalisation:** *extending the use of the language into the optimum range of social situations, i.e. the private sector, entertainment, sport and the media.*

Figure 6.6 Language survival: Five focii of social pressure for language change.
Source: Fishman (1991: 81)

where the decline in the use of Welsh is most apparent, because it's a very dense population area. The Gwendraeth valley is where you have practically the only coincidence of a dense population where the majority speak Welsh. So this has led to policies of government and local government support in this region.

What we're dealing with here is not bilingualism by individual practice; we're talking about bilingualism for, effectively, a whole culture. And it's an *indigenous* culture. This is based on Fishman's description of reversing language shift. In the view of Colin Williams from Stafford, language survival is a process in Wales which has gone through the five stages in Figure 6.6.

- From the *'idealism'* period, recognising that the language is threatened;
- going through a *'protest'* period, where you have agitation (and it's purely on behalf of the language itself, not the community);
- securing a generalised *'acceptance* of the *normalacy* of exercising language rights in *selected* domains';
- *'institutionalisation'* of the languages in key strategic agencies, law, education and public administration. These have been gained. People can be tried, before a court, in the Welsh language. What they can't get, yet, is a jury of 12 Welsh-speaking people. (They are tried by simultaneous translation.)

- 'Public administration' [picking up the document *Statistics of Education in Wales/Ystadegau Addysg yng Nghymru*]: it's bilingual only on the surface, because it costs too much to produce a document in two languages. Let me give you an example. [Picks up a slim volume.] That's the National Curriculum History Working Group Final Report. So that's History... in England. [Another document is shown, twice the thickness.] That's History in Wales, a separate document, because it was produced by the History Committee for Wales.

FROM THE FLOOR (FTF): Were there Welsh-speaking people engaged in producing that document?

WR: Well, they weren't *all* Welsh-speaking, but it was designed for the schools of Wales.

FTF: No, that's a different matter, whether it's designed for Wales. Did Welsh people write in that document?

WR: Oh, yes. It was a committee that was brought together from the schools and colleges of Wales. And only one member of the group writing the English document was present in the group writing the Welsh one.

FTF: Are those Welsh members very effective? Because here in England there are many people in different committees from ethnic minorities, but they are not very effective, because there are only one or two in a committee.

WR: Oh, I see, yes. That is an important issue. Their views are very often overridden, aren't they? Because they are in a very clear minority. And I met that situation only last week again, where one person wasn't able to get her views heard sufficiently, and had to accept what was the majority view, in one of these National Committees.

Back to Figure 6.6. If we're talking about '*normalisation*', which is the final stage in this process of gaining a place for the Welsh-speaking person on the world stage, we're talking about self-determination. That is: Who are they? What are they? How do they want to live?

An example of extending the use of the language into the private sector is to be seen on water vans in Wales. They're bilingual: on one side of the van is 'Dw'r Cymru'; on the other side is 'Welsh Water'.

Welsh has also been extended into entertainment and the media...

[WR starts the video. *Parablu*, by HTV, an educational programme intended for second-language learners of Welsh, begins to play.]

TV PRESENTER: I wonder if you've ever seen a caravan like this before? It's pulled by a large hairy thing called *Llew*. A group of actors live in this caravan. They travel from place to place, performing plays. They're called *y Carafanwyr*. This is Bleddyn, a very important member of this group. He writes the plays, and tells everyone what to do and how to say the words. They're all very keen to be in Bleddyn's plays. Sometimes, it's difficult for Bleddyn to choose the best actor for the part.

Y Carafanwyr all work very hard to learn the words they have to say. Here is Madam Llyr, learning her part for the next play. Sometimes, the actors need to wear special clothes to act in the plays. This is Dora's job.

Tilsli has an important job, too. He works at the back of the stage. He opens the curtains and changes the scenery.

[The tape is paused]

WR: One of the people involved in that was Jocelyn Stevens, who was involved in the American *Sesame Street*. They've gone to her because they want to reproduce the professionalism and attractiveness of what was obviously a very successful second-language series in the United States of America. That is American for Hispanics, and this is Welsh for English learners.

FTF: Do they go into Welsh, then?

WR: Oh yes. Let's fast-forward the video and see what we've got.

TV PRESENTER: Un, dau, tri, pedwar, pump, chwech, saith, wyth, naw, DEG! Da iawn. Nawr gyda miwsig, Madam Llyr!

[Y carafanwyr then sing '*un, dau, tri, pedwar, pump, chwech, saith, wyth, naw, deg*', accompanied by music from Madam Llyr, in order to practise their counting.]

FTF: It's a commercial company.

WR: It is. It's important that that kind of image is given to Welsh as a Second Language. That's Key Stage One, Welsh for ages 5 to 7. [*Holding up a large folder produced by HTV.*] Again, another very big document, because it's in Welsh on that side. But obviously, it's the English side that's going to be read by most of the teachers that are teaching that course, because they don't speak Welsh themselves.

So, it's in entertainment. HTV received half a million pounds two years ago to produce 24 programmes, so there's central government support. And there's also a professional team who are Welsh-speaking, brought together from the colleges and from the media, that can work both in Welsh and in English – so I should imagine that a lot of the professional side was done through the medium of Welsh, but a lot of the technical side of it would have been done through the medium of English. Nevertheless, there are movements afoot to train people who can work through the medium of Welsh in the media as well, in radio and television. We have S4C and we have Radio Cymru which are peopled by Welsh-speakers. So, what we are aiming for is Central Government supporting across the whole spectrum of educational, social and industrial development, and they want to work bilingually.

The situation of education in Wales, and its place in that whole process of making it 'normal', obviously takes you back to the 1988 Act. And in the 1988 Act, the Welsh Language was recognised as being an important part of the Curriculum. (See Figure 6.7.)

The core subjects are mathematics, English, science and, in relation to schools in Wales which are Welsh-speaking, Welsh. Now, that is in the National Curriculum in the Education Reform Act, so those of you who have looked at the actual Act will become aware, obviously, that there are extra provisions to do with Welsh, in Wales.

The other foundation subjects are history, geography, technology, music, art and physical education; in relation to third and fourth key stages, a modern foreign language, and, in relation to schools in Wales which are not Welsh-speaking schools, Welsh.

So there is a distinction between Welsh as a core subject and Welsh as a foundation subject. That was a very important consideration, that it should be included in the National Curriculum. But it wasn't included in the National Curriculum without a lot of lobbying; because the National Curriculum, as you are all very aware, doesn't deal with 'language', mathematics and science. And the fact that it doesn't deal with 'language', but with 'English', led to this kind of situation.

Let me show you what happened in the growth of Welsh-medium education during the 10, 15, 20 years up to 1988. Figure 6.8 is a graph showing the numbers of pupils who are able to speak Welsh, in the eight counties of Wales. The black section shows fluent speakers of Welsh who speak Welsh at home. The dark hatching shows pupils who speak Welsh fluently but do not speak it at home. The grey shading

The National Curriculum	2. The provisions of this Chapter shall have effect for the purpose of securing that there is implemented, as part of the curriculum for every maintained school, a basic curriculum for all registered pupils of compulsory school age (to be known as "the National Curriculum") which comprises the core and other foundation subjects and specifies in relation to each of them –

    (a) the knowledge, skills and understanding which pupils of different abilities and maturities are expected to have by the end of each key stage (in this Chapter referred to as "attainment targets");

    (b) the matters, skills and processes which are required to be taught to pupils of different abilities and maturities during each key stage (in this Chapter referred to as "programmes of study"); and

    (c) the arrangements for assessing pupils at or near the end of each key stage for the purpose of ascertaining what they have achieved in relation to the attainment targets for that stage (in this Chapter referred to as "assessment arrangements").

Foundation subjects and key stages.	3. (1) Subject to subsection (4) below, the core subjects are – (a) mathematics, English and science; and (b) in relation to schools in Wales which are Welsh-speaking schools, Welsh.

    (2) Subject to subsection (4) below, the other foundation subjects are –

    (a) history, geography, technology, music, art and physical education;

    (b) in relation to the third and fourth stages, a modern foreign language specified in an order of the Secretary of State; and

    (c) in relation to schools in Wales which are not Welsh-speaking schools, Welsh.

Figure 6.7 Education reform: Part I, Principal provisions.
Source: Education Reform Act, Chapter 40 (1988: 2)

shows pupils who speak Welsh but not fluently, and finally the lightest hatching shows those who do not speak Welsh at all.

So if you've got 30,000 pupils in the five to eleven age-group (primary schools) in Clwyd, the numbers of actual Welsh speakers are somewhere in the region of 3,000. Then if you look at South Glamorgan [De Morg], they almost disappear. And in Gwent, they *have* disappeared. You can't see the number of Welsh speakers, there are so few. The only areas that you can actually say have a strong population of Welsh-speaking children are the rural counties of Dyfed and Gwynedd, where you have many hundreds of children speaking Welsh. And that's in the period up to the present time, about two years ago.

What's happened over the last 20 years to try and change that situation? One of the most important things is the Mudiad Ysgolion Meithrin.

Nifer y plant / Number of children

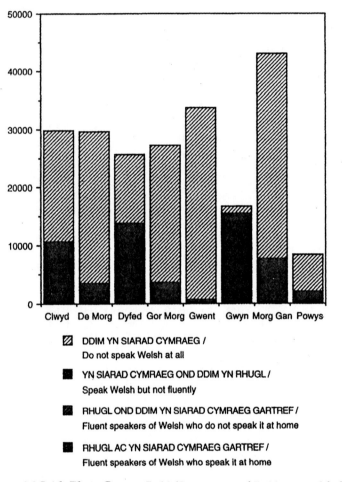

Figure 6.8 Iaith Plant Cymru 5–11/Language of 5–11-year-old children in Wales. Y Gallu I Siared Cymraeg (1989-90)/Ability to speak Welsh (1989–90).
Source: Swyddfa Gymreig/Welsh Office (1991)

Mudiad Ysgolion Meithrin is 'The Movement for Schools that Nurse'. So that's the three to fives. It's a voluntary organisation, Mudiad Ysgolion Meithrin: Nursery Schools Movement. There is no develop-ment, obviously, unless children are introduced to the language at a

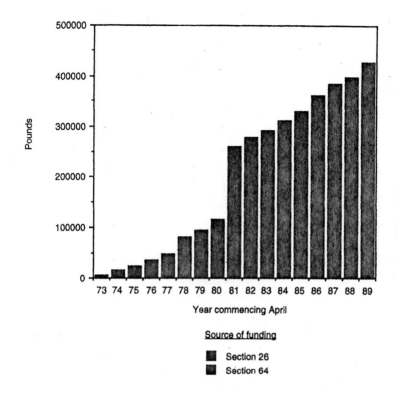

Figure 6.9 Mudiad Ysgolion Meithrin: Cyfanswm Grantiau'r Swyddfa Gymreig/Welsh-medium Nursery Schools Movement: Aggregate Support from Welsh Office 1973–89. Based on Mudiad Ysgolion Neithrin's Annual Report 1991

very young age, from two and a half onwards. They have received support from the Welsh Office since 1973, under the different Bills or Acts that enable them to do this, and it's gone up from less than £10,000 to over £400,000 in that 10 or 15 year period. (See Figure 6.9.)

FTF: What is the money going towards, then?

WR: It's going towards establishing a national office, with a director and office staff, and development officers in each of the eight authorities, and, on some occasions, two or three development officers, who assist the voluntary groups in running their activities in an effective way.

FTF: Is that bilingually, then?

WR: Well, the Movement themselves insist that it is monoglot Welsh.

FTF: Do they monitor standards?

WR: They try to, yes.

FTF: Because that would be important, wouldn't it?

WR: Of course, yes. It's the basis of BILINGUALISM – in order to establish bilingualism in young children, they have to *overlearn* the Welsh. It's the 'immersion' system.

FTF: Is there an allocation for the training of these teachers?

WR: No, not directly, because they are not teachers. They are nursery helpers and nursery leaders, and they can pay for their own training because they are voluntary. Or they can receive Social Security grants (under Employment Training, for example) if they follow certain language courses in Welsh L2. That's *my* job: to tell the Welsh Office to give them money for training.

FTF: So is there no statutory nursery education, then?

WR: Oh yes, but we're talking about the voluntary organisation where parents choose. The statutory provision is English-medium.

FTF: Why can't the statutory nursery provision be Welsh-medium?

WR: No, you can't do that! [*Mimicking local councillor.*] 'They're *our* schools. You can't take our schools, for Welsh-medium education!'

FTF: So what happens in the statutory nursery schools, then?

WR: In all the counties except Gwynedd and Dyfed, they're English-medium. 98%.

FTF: So the voluntary sector is having to work against that.

ANOTHER VOICE FROM THE FLOOR: It's like the community schools for community languages in England, where the Swann Report said that it's the job of the community to look after its languages, and the parents will pay for their children, to meet the cost, and provide a place in the gudwara or the mosque.

WR: Parents can now leave their children with the 800 groups of Mudiad Ysgolion Meithrin not just from three up, but also from two up. (See Figure 6.10.)?

FTF: In these 800 groups, how many children are being looked after by the ladies.

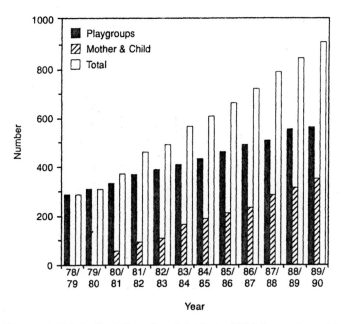

Figure 6.10 Mudiad Ysgolion Meithrin/Welsh-medium Nursery Schools Movement: Nifer Cychoedd/ Number of Groups 1979–90. Based on Mudiad Ysgolion Meithrin's Annual Report 1991

W.R. [*referring to Figure 6.11*]: In 1979/80 you had 4,600 children. And in 1989/90, there were 13,000. It's trebled in the 10 year period.

FTF: Is that instead of statutory school provision, or in addition to?

WR: Instead of. And cheaper than statutory school (See Figure 6.11).

As a result of the nursery school input, have come the Ysgolion Cynradd Dwyieithog Penodol: Designated Primary Bilingual Schools. Parents have said: 'My child isn't going to the local primary school; my child is going to *that* Welsh-medium school', which has been changed, under Section 12 or Section 13, from being an English-medium primary school to being a Welsh-medium primary school.

So the number of those schools has increased steadily. The first one was set up in about 1939 as a private school, and was taken over by the Local Authority in 1953. [*Referring to Figure 6.12*]: In 1950, there were less than 10 schools in a couple of Authorities, in 1960 it had trebled, and now, in 1989, there are about 13,000 pupils designated in Welsh-medium primary schools.

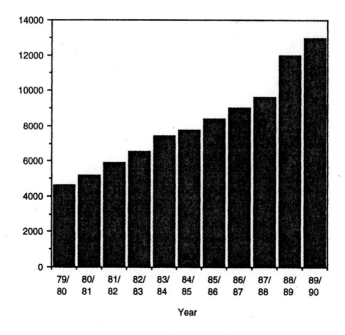

Figure 6.11 Mudiad Ysgolion Meithrin/Welsh-medium Nursery Schools Movement: Nifer Plant/Number of Children 1979–90. Based on Mudiad Ysgolion Meithrin's Annual Report 1991)

FTF: Are some schools likely to opt out, to avoid the changes?

WR: They may be forced to, if they are under LMS. Local governors can say: 'You're not taking *our* school. We'll opt out, rather than let you take *our* school'.

So that's going to become a great, great difficulty from now on: obtaining a site and staff that are prepared to change from being an English-medium school to becoming a Welsh-medium school. You could all be parents with young children, and you could say: 'Next September, we're all coming to *your* school, and we want it to become a Welsh-medium primary school'. And the governors could say: 'No, you're not having *our* school; and if the Local Authority want us to close so that you can become a Welsh-medium school, we'll opt out'.

And let's see what happens on the 9th of April. Up till now, they've been allowed to opt out. Tiny secondary schools of 230 pupils have opted out in Gwent because the Secretary of State for Wales has been happy for them to opt out.

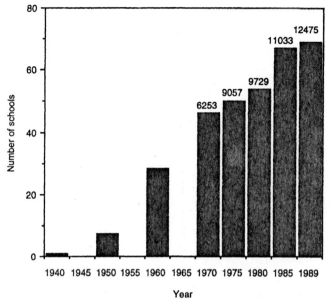

Figure 6.12 Ysgolion Cynradd Dwyieithog Penodol/Designated Primary Bilingual Schools. The figure at the top of each column from 1970 to 1989 represents the number of *pupils* Based on Swyddfa Gymreig/Welsh Office (1991).
Source: PDAG (May 1991)

FTF: To save the English.

WR: Oh yes.

FTF: The threatened English language!

WR: Because if they'd been closed, they would have become Welsh-medium schools immediately, the following week.

FTF: Is there a group or class of Welsh-speaking people, who think that if they send their children to Welsh-medium schools, their future won't be the same as if they send their children to English-speaking schools?

WR: Oh yes. That is the phrase: 'You need English to get on'. There are a lot of parents that, say, moved from rural parts of Wales in the last generation, who have children going through the system. And I have argued well into the night on many occasions with such parents who have said: 'Well, my children have gone to the nursery school with yours, and they can go on to the primary school with yours, but when they get into the secondary school, that's serious. I think they'll have to go to the local English-medium secondary school, then'.

FTF: Well why don't they have dual language, then? In the early 1970s, we had a choice of Geography lectures in English or Welsh, and that seemed to work.

WR: Oh yes. The choice available in Wales is quite considerable. I'll try to explain the different kinds of provision that are available.

WR: [Referring to Table 6.2:] If a school offers A, then they could offer B.

There are no schools in category B that offer A.

Table 6.2 Number of primary schools teaching through the medium of Welsh

		1986/87	1987/88	1988/89	1989/90	1990/91
A	Schools having classes where Welsh is the sole or main medium of instruction of first and second language pupils	358	363	368	417	445
	Percentage of schools	20.3	20.7	21.1	24.1	25.9
B	Schools having classes of first and second language pupils where some of the teaching is through the medium of Welsh	105	94	87	51	36
	Percentage of schools	6.0	5.4	5.0	2.9	2.1
C	Schools having classes of second language pupils where some of the teaching is through the medium of Welsh	122	136	133	129	122
	Percentage of schools	6.9	7.8	7.6	7.5	7.1
D	Schools having classes where Welsh is taughtas a second language but not used as a teaching medium	806	818	827	835	870
	Percentage of Schools	45.7	46.6	47.4	48.2	50.7
E	Schools where no Welsh is taught	371	343	331	299	244
	Percentage	21.1	19.5	18.9	17.3	14.2
	Total	1762	1754	1746	1731	1718

Source: Swyddfa Gymreig/Welsh Office (1991: 89)

There are no schools in category C that offer B or A.

There are no schools in category E that offer any of those above.

Let's start at the bottom. E is schools where no Welsh is taught, even as a first language or as a second language, where the Education Reform Act told them that Welsh is a part of the curriculum as a core or foundation subject. So that's now illegal. They're being given a dispensation for an extra year or two to get the staff. [See Table 6.3]

D is schools having classes where Welsh is taught as a Second Language, but not used as a teaching medium. We'll look at the balance of this later.

FTF: And these mean schools from Infant – five years – up?

WR: Yes. From Reception, effectively. In fact, in D and E you are talking about children at the age of three, because they are in English-medium nursery provision.

C is schools having classes of second language pupils. You're talking about Cardiff, and Wrecsam on the industrial east, where some of the teaching is through the medium of Welsh – where their parents say: 'Oh, they can have an afternoon of Welsh, every day'. So they send their

Table 6.3 Timetable for implementing the recommendations of the 1988 Act

Academic Year	Schools where Welsh is taught Key Stages				Schools where Welsh is not taught Key Stages			
	1	2	3	4	1	2	3	4
1990/91	5/9	7/8	11/12					
1991/92	6/7	8/9	12/13					
1992/93		9/10	13/14		5/6		11/12	
1993/94		10/11		14/15	6/7		12/13	
1994/95				15/16		7/8	13/14	
1995/96						8/9		14/15
1996/97						9/10		15/16
1997/98						10/11		

Based on information from Swyddfa Gymreig/Welsh Office
Source: PDAG (April 1991: 1)

children there, and they do all their maths and English in the morning, and they do their history and geography in Welsh in the afternoon, or a little bit of art and craft through Welsh in the afternoon.

The schools in category B have classes of first and second language pupils, so you've now got a combination of first and second language pupils. Parents who come to live in Wales say: 'I want my children to have Welsh-medium bilingual education', so they go into the same schools or classes as children from homes where they speak Welsh at home. So *those* children are in a total immersion situation; the other children are in a home-language situation; and they are being taught together, with no distinction.

And then, obviously, the A category is most of the schools in Gwynedd and Dyfed, where there are classes, though not necessarily *all* classes, where Welsh is the sole or main medium of instruction – medium of *instruction*, note! And I must admit that one of my themes when I was an Inspector of Schools in Gwynedd was that when they were teaching English as a subject, in primary schools, they didn't use enough English. So they weren't really giving them English language experiences.

So what they're getting in some parts of Wales is English Language through the medium of Welsh. And maybe there's a reason for that... [Holds up another large bound volume.] That is a document which is in Draft 5, produced by the Advisory Service in Gwynedd Local Authority and it's to do with developing Literacy in the Early Years. The whole document describes good practice as far as the Local Authority is concerned, and it says, for example, that the teacher's main task is to find out where the children are and to carry on from that point. What experience do they bring with them, in other words? What have they already learned before the teachers meet them? It concerns the diagnosis, the assessment, before they start, effectively. But the whole document doesn't refer once to 'Cymraeg' and it doesn't refer *once* to 'English'. It just refers to 'Literacy'. It deals with literacy as a process, as a phenomenon; it doesn't refer to any specific language. And I think that's a policy decision. They don't want to distinguish between literacy in English and literacy in Welsh, but that has the implication that they ignore the distinction between English and Welsh; that they don't deal with them as bilingual children, necessarily, because they want to deal with them as monoglot Welsh as much as possible.

FTF: That has its down side.

WR: Of course it has. It has a very important down side.

FTF: That's almost the English model. That's what they do in England.

ANOTHER VOICE FROM THE FLOOR: Are there any children or adults who might find it very difficult or don't speak any English?

WR: They're in their 80s. But you can appreciate that people who have been natural Welsh-speakers all their lives, but who have used English in their professional or in their working life – once they reach the age of 40 or 50 when they are no longer required in industry, then they will return to their home situation and everything will be in Welsh from then on. And if, for any reason, they become senile – even prematurely senile – they then aren't able to express themselves in English any more. And this is a *great* problem for the caring professions.

Any child up to six or seven really needs to be dealt with, to be effective, in Welsh – and anybody coming to the *end* of their active life needs to be dealt with in their first language. And the caring professions need to be very aware of this, and *trained* to respond to it.

And what came out in 1989? The Children Act. One of the basic provisions of the Children Act is that clients need to be dealt with in their most comfortable language. It's a very important issue for you. You could bring out the Children Act as evidence more often than the Education Act.

[Referring to Table 6.4:] In Wales, there's a total of 1,700 primary schools with a total of 256,000 pupils. There are 417 Welsh-speaking primary schools, with 45,000 pupils. There are also 417 schools that are

Table 6.4 Ysgolion Cymru/Schools in Wales 1989–90

Ysgolion Cynradd/Primary Schools	Ysgolion/Schools	Disgyblion/Pupils
Cyfanswm ysgolion Cymru/ Total in Wales	1,729 (100%)	256,878 (100%)
Ysgolion 'siarad Cymraeg'/ Welsh-medium schools	417 (24%)	45,387 (18%)
Addysg yn bennaf drwy'r Gymraeg/ Schools teaching primarily through the medium of Welsh	417 (24%)	36,441 (14%)

Based on Swyddfa Gymreig/Welsh Office (1991)

working primarily through the medium of Welsh, but there are only 36,000 pupils being taught primarily through the medium of Welsh. This means that there is a distinct difference, of 9,000 pupils, between those that are *in* Welsh-medium schools and those that are being taught primarily through the medium of Welsh. So there are 9,000 pupils that are not in *designated* Welsh schools, but in Welsh-speaking schools – because there are *natural* Welsh-speaking schools, as well as designated Welsh-speaking schools – who are not actually following most of their education through the medium of Welsh. In other words, you as a class teacher, have got 13 Welsh-speaking pupils and 12 English-speaking pupils, and you're doing History with them, or you're doing Topic with them. So there are practical problems that arise out of that kind of natural Welsh-speaking school. And it's the view of parents that a school with that kind of mixture of children (categories A and B in Table 6.2), unless it's fully supported, can be very inefficient, in small rural primary schools. It can also be very, very worrisome for teachers, because they don't feel that they're providing the *best* situation for their children.

So there's tremendous pressure at the present time in two directions: one, to designate schools as 'Welsh-medium', which means that every child going to them will receive most of their education through the medium of Welsh and is expected to become fully fluent in Welsh; and there's another pressure for people who live in places like Dyfed to actually provide monoglot English schools for their pupils, because 'Education comes first, not Language'. This is the same kind of pressure that people in Quebec are having from English-speaking Canadians who say 'We live in Quebec, but we don't want to speak French', and the same kind of pressure that you have in places like South Africa, with Afrikaans, and the kind of pressures that people in the Basque country are having from Spaniards who don't want to learn Basque in order to live there; people who live in Catalonia who don't want to speak Catalan, they want to speak Spanish; such as you have in places like Estonia and Lithuania, where people want to speak Russian rather than Estonian or Lithuanian because they've lived there and spoken Russian for the last 50 years.

So there are English-speaking people who buy a little house in Dyfed for £20,000, having sold their house for £80,000 in London, who want to find an English-medium primary school for their children in Dyfed. But there are only 10 children living within 10 miles, anyway. Now, you're the teacher responsible for them, and you have eight children that are learning their National Curriculum subjects through the medium of Welsh, and one family arrives, and you've now got 16 children. That's

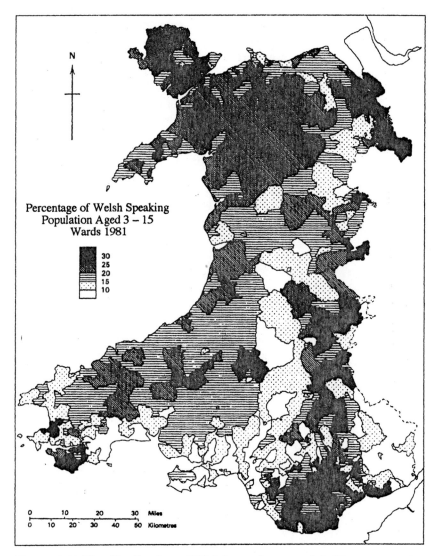

Figure 6.13 The distribution of Welsh speakers aged 3–15 as proportions of those speaking Welsh, 1981.
Source: Aitchison & Carter (1985: Map 10)

the practical situation, and some of the answers are interesting...

In Figure 6.13 the darkest areas. It's in those areas, the industrialised areas of the east and south-east that the percentage of *school age* Welsh speakers is highest – over 30% – as a proportion of those speaking Welsh. The Heartland areas are 15% to 20%. The significant thing is that when you have over 30%, you're talking about *increase* in knowledge of the Welsh language, and the increases in knowledge of the Welsh language for young children aged 3 to 15 are in the Anglicised areas – and that's the result of the Education system.

The evidence has come through in the 1981 Census that the only *growth* in the Welsh-speaking population that has taken place in the last 50 years, perhaps 80 years, is in the Anglicised areas – as a result of the Education system. And we're hoping that the 1991 Census will show an even greater growth in the speaking of Welsh. In Taf Elái, in the Pontypridd area of south-east Wales, 25% of the population go to designated Welsh-medium schools, and all those children come from homes that are English-speaking. This is because their grandparents didn't speak Welsh to their parents, so the parents want their children to have Welsh back. The only way they can get it back is by sending them to school. It's a maintenance problem.

FTF: Is there professional concern about the early years learning, about the situation of children who are being educated at school at 4, 5 and 6 through the medium of Welsh, but whose home language is English, as you've just described – in that they're disadvantaged as compared with their classmates who have Welsh at home and at school, and who have a unified experience?

WR: Yes, that is a very great concern.

FTF: Have you any comment about that? Because that parallels with the children whose home language is different from the school language in other places?

WR: The concern is, I think, based upon the understanding that Jim Cummins has transferred to all of us of the threshold levels of competence, and that children who are not brought up to a level of competence in their second language (which is the language of the school) comparable to their home language, are not going to have a positive, interactive bilingualism – and therefore it's very important that the schools identify those children having difficulty in their second language and give them extra support. And the schools are geared up to do that.

FTF: They are?

WR: Oh yes. Nevertheless, it's very easy for parents to blame the school for the lack of success that their own children are having, and it's then incumbent on the teachers to point out that the children wouldn't have gained any more success academically in the one language if they'd been taught through the medium of the mother tongue the whole time. And that's a very difficult point to make to parents, that they wouldn't have been more effective as learners, even if they had been learning through their mother tongue.

The important thing to consider is that there is not a single teacher working in a Welsh-medium situation who isn't bilingual. *They are all fluent in English.* They have all passed 'O' Level English as well as 'O' Level Maths. So there is no child in any school in Wales that comes from an *English-speaking* background that cannot be understood when they want to make a point showing understanding. That is the *crucial* difference between the situation with Welsh in Wales and the situation you find yourselves in in England.

FTF: And that's the crucial point about the immersion system in Canada. The way it works turns on this crucial point that *all* Canadian French-speaking teachers understand English for their English-speaking children.

WR: They do. And the children *know* that they understand English.

ANOTHER VOICE: That's the point at which many of us would like to know about the *other languages of Wales.*

W.R.: Yes. I couldn't get any information about it from the book of *Statistics of Educational Provision in Wales.* I was in the company of language advisers from the eight authorities on Thursday and Friday. Now, these are the Welsh language advisers for counties like Gwynedd, Dyfed, South Glamorgan and Gwent, and I asked them: 'Are there any schools that receive Section 11 Grants? Does the Authority have a team of people working under Section 11?' They said: 'Section 11? What do you mean?'

These are the language advisers, for Welsh. Their whole professional life is engaged in this struggle of establishing the Welsh language dimension. And it has not yet hit... the Welsh Office, let's say – it hasn't hit most of the counties in Wales – that there are *other* languages, wider language dimensions, which need to be addressed.

The only adviser that responded at all was for the authority in Gwent, which is the one closest to Gloucestershire, opposite Bristol.

And in the Gwent authority they are discussing their finances for the next financial year this week. Obviously, they've only got their plans in place and they've only heard this week exactly how much money they are going to get. And the Welsh language adviser heard last week that the authority want to appoint a team of 16 support teachers to deal with the problems of schools in the inner-city areas, where they have anything up to 20 or 30 different home languages. And her response was: 'How can the Authority give that kind of level of priority to funding *those* posts when I in Gwent have a National Curriculum requirement to teach Welsh to every single child in the County, and I only have 20 first-language speakers on my staff?' And she has therefore spent the last fortnight trying to persuade the authority to transfer the funding from *that* area of the Curriculum to *her* area.

FTF: Was this funding directed towards English support, or Welsh?

WR: It was English as a Second Language. That's the whole point about it. Now, there are schools that receive support under Section 11, certainly, in South Glamorgan and in Gwent, but these support teams have not yet been developed as you're familiar with them, and I actually couldn't find out from the Welsh Office how much grant support is given to the counties of Wales – so it's a *hidden question* at the present time.[1]

FTF: The linguistic demands for children from an ethnic minority background are huge. If you have a child whose mother tongue is, say, Panjabi, the requirement in Wales is for that child to learn Welsh, and to function, that child is going to need to speak English. The linguistic demands are *enormous*.

WR: Huge, yes.

Note

1. In September 1992, Bill Raybould contacted the Welsh Office to ascertain:
   (i)   whether LEAs in Wales receive Section 11 support from the Welsh Office,
   (ii) what the nature is of any work undertaken in Wales with Section 11 support, including how many 'community languages', schools, pupils or LEA staff are involved.

In answer to (i), the following statement was made:

In the financial year 1992/93, in Wales, project applications were made by Cardiff City Council, Gwent County Council, South Glamorgan County Council and Gwynedd County Council. Seven project applications were successful and all but Gwynedd County Council had projects approved.

It was also added that Cardiff City Council and South Glamorgan Council are 'the only two authorities which have received grant in Wales from 1982/1983 financial year to date'. (Gwent County Council had three project applications approved for funding from April 1992, but no payment had been made at the time of the letter (30.9.92) as posts were not yet filled.)

In answer to (ii), the only reply offered was:

S11 grant is administered by the Home Office for England and Wales. It is designed to address the needs of those individuals from the new commonwealth who, for reasons of language or culture, are prevented from gaining access to mainstream local authority provision and who are consequently disadvantaged. Typically this is addressed through support for ESL teaching in schools.

References

Aitchison, J. and Carter, H. (1985) *The Welsh Language 1961–1981: An Interpretative Atlas.* Cardiff: University of Wales Press.

Cummins, J. (1979) Cognitive/academic language proficiency, linguistic interdependence, the optimum age question and some other matters. *Working Papers on Bilingualism* No. 19, 121–9.

Department of Education and Science (1988) *Education Reform Act.* London: HMSO.

Fishman, J.A. (1991) *Reversing Language Shift.* Clevedon: Multilingual Matters.

Pryce, W. T. R. (1978) Welsh and English in Wales 1750–1971: A spatial analysis based on the linguistic affiliation of parochial communities. *Bulletin of the Board of Celtic Studies* XXVIII (1), 1–36. Cardiff: University of Wales Press.

Pwyllgor Datblygu Addysg Gymraeg (Welsh Language Education Development Committee) April 1991, *Y Gymraeg yn y Cwricwlwm Cenedlaethol: Cyflenwad Athrawon [Welsh in the National Curriculum: Supply of Teachers].* Cardiff: PDAG.

—(May 1991) *Y Gymraeg yn Ysgolion Cymru: Ystadegau [Welsh in the Schools of Wales: Statistics].* Cardiff: PDAG.

Welsh Office (1991) *Statistics of Education in Wales: Schools* No.5. Cardiff.

Williams, C.H. and Raybould, W.H. (1991) *Welsh Language Planning: Opportunities and Constraints.* Contribution to Seminario Internacional sobre Planificación Lingüística (Santiago de Compostela), transactions in press. Extract published by PDAG, Cardiff.

7 Issues in the Language Education of Bilingual Children: Summary of the Open Forum for Participants' Contribution

MAHENDRA K. VERMA, KAREN P. CORRIGAN and SALLY FIRTH

This plenary session was organised to provide an opportunity for the course participants to discuss issues which were of importance to them. The aim of the session was to allow further discussion of any of the issues which had been raised during the four days of the course, or to introduce any matters which had not been addressed at all. The participants were invited to put forward their own questions, concerns and opinions. The session is presented here as an edited transcript. This format was chosen to ensure accurate representation of the contributors' views. It is followed by a summary of the discussion.

Key

A =Chair

B = Bilingual Support Teacher

C = Mainstream Class Teacher

D = Co-ordinator of an English Language Support Service

E = Primary Teacher Trainer

F = Support Teacher

G = Director of the Welsh Language Education Development Committee

H = Postgraduate Researcher and ESL Teacher

I = Support Teacher

94

A: My first question is not to elicit information, but to elicit ideas and reactions. We have heard what is happening in Wales; we have also had a chance to look at the initiatives taken in Lothian. In Scotland the curriculum is different from Wales. Wales has the most elaborate one, and on the surface it is the most generous – but only to the *indigenous* minorities there. It is very generous, and I have always said that that document is a *landmark*. However, it has also created a lot of problems and issues. For example, it states that the reason why the government has recognised the importance of Welsh in Wales (and the models of first language/second language/extended second language and the rest of the possibilities) is because Wales is a *nation*. They have raised the issue of territorial rights, then.

In England, they have raised the issue of entitlement of all children, but not territorial entitlement. Territorial entitlement is only relevant to people who are supposed to be all English people. We are all familiar with the fact that in the Kingman and Cox Reports 'language' means 'English'. It always refers to English.

The territorial integrity of Wales has been recognised, then. The language rights that follow the principle of territorial integrity have also been recognised. This has led us into the debate of whether there is an equation between land, people and language. If a community exists which perceives itself as a community, but which does not have, politically, a piece of land (except in amusing and political jargon like 'Leicester is a little Gujerat', 'Bradford is a little Pakistan', and 'Southall is a little Panjab'), their territorial rights are not the rights that at least I consider to be important when we come to consider the education of children. It doesn't matter whether a child has got any relationship with the name of the area that he or she is actually growing up in. If it did matter, a Panjabi child not living in Panjab would have no rights, for example. It doesn't matter if your community is not recognised historically – it's not relevant.

We talk about bilingual *support* or language *support*. Does this mean (a) supporting and developing children's bilingualism, or (b) simply helping them with their English? Or do we believe in what the Welsh voluntary group is doing, as well as what the statutory bodies are doing: literacy in the mother tongue, at an early stage? Because this would lay the foundation for later, when they moved on to English. Literacy in the mother tongue is important for literacy in the second language.

B: What we're talking about is the difference between *bilingual teaching*, which is what eventually will come in Wales, and *bilingual support*, which is what the Home Office want *us* to do. It's permanent bilingualism versus transitional bilingualism. The point is that it doesn't matter how good *we* want it to be, because it depends whether the political masters let it be done.

A: But it is important. Even if laws and statutes don't allow you to do certain things because you have to deliver a curriculum, do you believe that that is what you should do?

B: Ideally it should be bilingual teaching, but I don't know that we have the resources to do that – the will is there, but the ability isn't.

C: What is on offer is going to differ for those of us who are not bilingual in the way we approach what we do. It obviously makes a difference.

A: Do you not think that there could be a partnership? You are a valuable teacher, whether you are an English monolingual teacher or a bilingual teacher. Do you not foresee that there could be better work in terms of methodology for a team who are always in partnership? Invariably it seems that the main classroom teacher *is* a monolingual English teacher, so couldn't the focus of the support teacher's role and the class teacher's role be integrated into something which goes together to the child?

B: The answer is to have more mainstream bilingual teachers.

C: Yes, I agree. Schools have a lot to do as well. We should also take some responsibility in training the people who are entering the profession. In our school, we recently used some of our LMS to bring in ancillaries who speak the mother tongue. They are not very well-equipped in English, but it is our duty to pull them along with us. And we have found that in a year the benefits have been absolutely tremendous. I think that we, as a *school*, have to take some of that responsibility. And as an *ordinary* class teacher, I have seen another side of things in hearing from the support service, which I didn't know a lot about before.

D: The issue is also linked in a very complex way to parental views, because without that kind of articulation– and therefore a kind of focus based on that articulation – it is very difficult to make any kind of bilingualism work. Because we see within our communities in Britain a whole range of feelings. For example, some parents say to their children: 'Don't ever speak Panjabi in school, because we want you to learn English'. This constitutes very powerful motivation. If you then place a child in direct conflict with that parental advice, insisting on using a bilingual approach (whatever that may mean), it would create all kinds of emotional problems as well as the obvious fall-out in educational terms for that child.

One of the things we ought to be concerned about in the future is *that* – not in a very high level, abstract kind of way, but actually to think in terms of how you articulate parental views at a school level and formulate a school policy on *that* basis. This is very important, but it is not an abstract issue of what we should do in England, because that can *not* be answered by *us*.

E: On a different point, I think that at the time when bilingual support teachers or bilingual support NTAs are appointed, there should be a brief as to what their duties are. For example, is their duty to teach the mother tongue? Because in my area, some teachers were very adamant that they would teach the mother tongue whether the authorities said so or not. But they also support English, as well as teach the mother tongue, so their job title is no longer adequately descriptive of their job. They are no longer bilingual support; they are parental involvement/ curriculum involvement support. Unless we know what our brief is and what other people's briefs are, it is very difficult to know our position, because of the confusion which has been created by the authorities.

A: That is one of the things our research project is carrying out. We are requesting all Heads of Service to let us have copies of job descriptions. This will inform us what the support teachers are being told to do.

F: I thoroughly approve of the idea of bilingual classrooms and of the idea of bilingual teachers – or two teachers, one of whom speaks language A and one of whom speaks language B, who are operating as equal colleagues. *But* it can't be done, productively, in my circumstances. It can't be done because there are simply too many languages in each class. Even if we looked at one school in the area where some 70–80% of the pupils speak Moroccan Arabic as their first language, I would still question whether we could set up a bilingual learning situation for those children. What would happen to the three Bengali speakers in the class? Would we say to them: 'This is not an appropriate school for you to attend, although it is your local school, because this is a bilingual *Arabic*-English school'. Or: 'You can come along and you can get the English, but it can be made clear to you at the same time that *your* language is a *third*-class language'.

If your client group is either monolingual English-speaking or language X-speaking, then you perhaps ought to be looking at this as a solution. But I feel very strongly that this situation is going to attain less and less, because people *do* move around. Traditionally, we are the area of London in which the Filipinos lived – but pupils are now beginning to move, to disperse themselves further. So Tower Hamlets, which is traditionally a Bengali area, now has Filipino pupils. As we must take the needs of *all* of the pupils seriously, I'm not sure that the bilingual education approach is going to be productive across the board.

A: There are two issues here. The first is that we have been using the term 'bilingual education approach' and it's not *one* kind of bilingual education approach. We may be talking about mother tongue support, and mother tongue development, but not mother tongue as a *medium*. We may use it *initially* as a medium at the point of entry for the child – when the child has no other language – and then gradually move towards English as the medium (still giving the mother tongue plenty of support).

D's point was about parental involvement. In a school where 80% of the children are Moroccan Arabic-speaking and only two or three Bengali-speaking, parental involvement will be *more* useful.

The other point I'd like to comment on is that there are isolated children in North Yorkshire, in Humberside and in Gateshead, where individual schools are predominantly English children. So imagine the Moroccan children to be like the English children and you've got one or two other children. And what is the policy of the authority? They have peripatetic teachers. So if each peripatetic teacher is to be justified, then in that predominantly Moroccan school, there could be a *peripatetic* teacher for those two or three Bangladeshi children, who would look after their mother tongue – alongside English, which they would be doing with the Moroccan children. The point I am trying to make is that although there are complexities, there are also possibilities.

There are further possibilities if we incorporate the idea of partnership teaching. Years ago in the Language Teaching Centre in this Department, Hawkins had an innovative idea. It constituted a one-to-one partnership for learning and teaching. He got in touch with lots of French teachers of English as a Second or Foreign Language in France, and English teachers teaching French in this country. He used to have a summer school of two or three weeks, and there was a one-to-one pairing: a French teacher who wanted to improve her English, or methodology and technique, came to England for this experience – and the English teacher teaching French was here with them and then went over to France. And it worked, for many years. It was a very good way for the French teacher to develop her expertise in English, *and* to transfer her skills in French, her mother tongue, to the English teacher.

Now in a similar way, couldn't the ancillary staff or the bilingual assistant (non-trained teachers) and the bilingual support English monolingual teacher embark on (with the will and money) a course where the monolingual English support teacher could begin to learn the language of the children? You might protest that there are too many languages. While that argument is relevant, it is not relevant to the extent that we want it to dismiss all the ideas about children's entitlements, and facilitation in their early years through their mother tongue. Because there *are* schools, such as the Moroccan school or schools in Bradford, Leeds, Leicester and Birmingham, which have got 99% of one language group – like Mirpuri Panjabi in Bradford, where one monolingual English child is in a minority.

If we as ESL teachers are so concerned about the mother tongue and the mother tongue resource, then make it a possibility for putting on an intensive two or three week course in the language and culture of the children. I am always misunderstood when I make any comment about language awareness courses so I'll be very careful. I do not wish this two or three week intensive course to be like a language awareness or language taster course -- but a *serious* course, where you go through this experience of learning another language. My wife and I used to do three-week summer courses in Leicester for ESOL teachers and it was very successful. Of course it came to an end because of lack of funding – but during those years I remember all the ESOL teachers who came onto the course really enjoyed it and made an effort. And if you *had* such courses, I think partnership would be a much better issue.

B: One of the problems with bilingual teaching and the lack of recognition of the teachers, especially the Asian ones, is *status*. Is there a link between low status and having teachers who are not *equally* fluent but competent users of both languages?

A: It's like a leopard being defined by its number of spots -- claiming that if it has one less spot then it is not a leopard. That is a definition which clearly won't work. The same goes for fluency and bilinguals. Remember that bilingual support teacher in Ann Hindle's video. I commented that she spoke beautiful Scottish Urdu – she was born here, and she studied Urdu, but the child's Urdu was better than her Urdu. But I don't think that is as important; what is important in my mind is that she *had* Urdu. Ann *did* say, to be fair to that teacher, that she wasn't *ready* for that kind of filming because she had never used Urdu. But it was used for the film so that later on they could use this strategy as much as possible. So although this teacher wasn't very experienced in using that mother tongue strategy, it might have done her good – to raise *her* consciousness: here was a fluent Urdu-speaking child and she (the teacher) grew up in this country, and can *speak* Urdu. I would like to dismiss those people who follow the idea of deceptive fluency – because one can become literate or one can become more proficient. So that could have good dividends – if it is done sensitively and carefully.

B: One of the problems is that sometimes you hear being said of bilingual teachers: 'She doesn't speak very good English, how can we employ her?'

A: I can tell you of an authority, without naming it, which trained some ethnic minority teachers for primary schools, and after three or four years, when 10 or 12 teachers graduated with PGCEs, messages came back from primary school head teachers such as: 'Well they can't apply for jobs in our schools' – and these were teachers who had done *teacher practice* in those schools – 'because their English is not very good'. The *partnership* strategy would help them. If you are learning Urdu from them, you can help them with their English.

B: It has worried me that the comment you hear about these PGCE graduates is: 'They will be very useful in schools with children from *their* cultural background'. It's as if they are OK for bilingual children but not the best for other children – which worries me.

E: I have two points in answer to A. Firstly, when those headteachers were asked what was wrong with their English, they said that they leave out the article ('a', 'an' and 'the'), and sometimes one or two other things. But there are different varieties of English, all over England – and in Yorkshire, people don't include 'the' all the time. Now I live in Yorkshire, so shall I call myself Yorkshire when I miss out 'the'?!

Secondly, it is *meaning* which should be put across to the children. It is the meaning which should be there in language. If I am able to put my meaning across to the children, then I think I am doing my job – if I leave out 'a' and 'the', I don't think it matters a lot. *Nobody* who is a second language speaker can be as perfect as a *first* language speaker in that language.

If *my* education had been in private school, perhaps I'd have said: 'Yes, my English is perfect English, and I speak R.P.'. But my education has been through state school in India, and that's where I learnt English. Then it was polished in this country. So I would say that I speak average English and people understand me – and that's the job of the language.

D: This is a question for G. In your experience in the recruitment of teachers for Welsh-medium schools, have you had any instances where a particular teacher is judged to be not very proficient in Welsh – because the racism element doesn't exist there, I hope. Does it occur?

[G nods.]

D: And what is done in that sort of situation – they don't get a job?

G: Not necessarily – they *do* get a job.

D: Right. So there is a clear bit of racism going on here, in England.

H: And is it not the case even outside education and the public service in Wales, that you are not disqualified by only being a beginner in a language – you are in fact *funded* to take a course, often at university or college.

G: This is why questions of *language* qualification in Wales are not race issues. The Racial Equality Act is not applicable when a person is barred from something because they're not bilingual – because it's not something that is done.

H: But people are actually funded to go on courses.

G: Oh yes.

H: That is unique to Wales – within Britain.

G: It is because the local authorities recognise it as a *growth* situation, and the only way in which they can improve the provision is to do this.

H: And they want more people to speak good Welsh. Do the English want more people to speak good English?!

G: You are still only talking about a certain kind of person in Wales.

H: I'm talking about the local authorities.

G: Oh yes, these are the people who are in charge of the provision.

H: They have got the *money*.

G: They have *some* money, and they want to use it in that way. They will train their teachers and they will train their workers. The most encouraging signs I have seen recently have been when I've been talking to people – for instance, people who work for the Curriculum Council of Wales. I had been talking to one person in a meeting for half an hour before realising that she was from Kent. She had been working for three years in a Welsh authority and operated through the medium of Welsh wherever she was in Wales. And that was simply the peer pressure of teachers in the schools where she was working; they just insisted on speaking Welsh with her, and she wanted to respond and took courses in Welsh.

H: Welsh people are very supportive of the learner. There is a climate of: 'You want to learn our language? How can we help?'.

G: Maybe so. Nevertheless learners will complain that Welsh-speaking people don't give them the support they want. You are talking about the *professional* group of people who see that it breeds equality –

whereas people who use Welsh as a matter of course, where it is a mere accident that they are Welsh-speaking, like to use their Welsh as an exclusive badge as well.

A: I saw a film last year about a mixed family of an English person and his West Indian wife who wanted their children to learn Welsh. And they said that there are Welsh speakers who say: 'You don't have to bother learning our language, you are quite OK with English'.

E: It is a problem. Because many Urdu and Bengali speakers don't want their language to be learned. And they don't want to *teach* their language.

A: Are there English people who identify themselves as English, who have been in Wales a couple of years and who are teaching Welsh?

G: Yes.

A: What percentage?

G: A small percentage. But in the situation we are now in, you have to distinguish between *indigenous* non-Welsh speakers (because they have lost their language over many generations) and recent arrivals. And the response of those two different groups is markedly different. There is obviously a great reluctance on the part of the indigenous population of Wales to recognise that they are themselves second-class citizens in their own country, and will not accept that they should learn to speak Welsh; whereas new arrivals look upon it as being a challenge and begin to learn Welsh. So there is a lot of social inertia.

H: In terms of languages in Wales, I saw an interesting article in the *Times Education Supplement* about Japanese. Now why is the Japanese language being taught?

A: It is 'commercially valid', in the words of the Cox Report.

H: That presumably *is* the thrust. The Welsh system has obviously responded to this. But is that Japanese being taught in the mainstream?

G: It is being taught to small groups of linguistically able pupils in schools based in Cardiff. Support teachers and other teachers are being put in at great expense to add another language to that school's list.

A: Shall we move on to another area: last year's SATs. Of those of you who took part in them, what role did you play?

B: I was a language support teacher. I concentrated on the speaking, which I know is not compulsory but the school I was in was 80% bilingual children, so it was important to monitor.

Our results tied in with the national trend: they did actually do quite well in science. Interestingly enough, they matched pretty well with Teacher Assessment as well – because they went to a school where the *ethos* is right. In contrast, in another school where we were supporting just three children, and where the teachers had a completely different attitude, the children didn't do very well in the SATs, even when they were helped bilingually – because of the way they were *taught*. This shouldn't happen.

G: Could I ask you to *define*, as briefly as possible, what you do as a bilingual teacher in that contact.

B: It's a support role. In one school, lessons are very often in dual language – so that a lesson could easily be introduced in Panjabi and followed with work in English. The small group work takes place in a multilingual situation. Children choose which language they want to operate in. It's the ideal.

G: Are both languages understood by the adults?

B: Well, four languages are being used: Panjabi, Urdu, Gujerati and English.

G: Do the adults who are in that situation understand all four languages?

B: No. Each situation has a Panjabi or an Urdu speaker.

G: The question I want to clear in my own mind is whether or not individual children were able to say what they understood clearly and have *that* understood (in SATs).

B: Yes.

G: Because it is the meaning coming from the children that is crucial. And that needs to be given its full weight in the education process.

B: They do it carefully, to make sure. So, for example, monolingual English teachers doing the science did not assess any of the children who we knew switched code. But she did assess some that were very fluent in English.

G: That is the crucial question in Wales: that the ṢATs should be assessed in the language the child offers.

B: Doing it by language need.

G: But the actual *achievement* in core subjects like maths and science can be vastly different from their achievement in the language, in English.

I: We had to do the whole lot in English.

G: So you weren't able to assess the understanding of the pupils.

I: Mm.

G: So these assessments, under monolingual conditions, were totally incorrect – by definition: they don't assess what the children know.

I: It's a very haphazard arrangement anyway. I was there; I was used. And I knew that the children *understood*, but they couldn't produce the English.

B: I was discussing this with a bilingual colleague who was also involved in another school: she felt that she got more out of the children than the monolingual class teacher. This was because her *questioning* technique was geared to the children's understanding. So you've got the double problem– not just that the children don't contribute; very often they haven't understood the question. Although we can say that the monolingual teacher *didn't* succeed, a carefully *trained* monolingual teacher will succeed more.

A: That is where the monolingual support teacher's role comes in – because she knows the child best.

G: I'd just like to make one final point. It came up when I was listening to Ann Robson yesterday and I suppose we've just been discussing the Cummins framework. The words that *I* put on the four cardinal points were *embodied* and *disembodied,* and *familiar* and *unfamiliar.* Because for me the crucial thing is that children associate language and person: language is *spoken,* and they associate a language with a person. If the language is embodied, then the child can understand it because the meaning is negotiated between the bodies. If it is disembodied you can't negotiate. The basis of meaning is negotiated between people, and they come to an understanding together. And that's what education is: getting to the same point of understanding.

So if the language is embodied, it is of an accessible nature. Obviously it's familiar. I think those two axes (of the Cummins framework) are more *human.* And they're two axes of the *same thing.*

H: In the Orders for Welsh in the National Curriculum in Key Stage 1, Reading, there is no mention of the acquisition of reading regular speech phonemes. There is none of this technological breakdown which is used in the English syllabus. There is a stress on listening to stories, retelling stories: the oral component in *reading* is *huge.* To lay the two Orders together, side by side, is amazing. And the Orders for Welsh as a *Second Language* are even more helpful in the structures which support reading: the *writing* and reading, the transcribing of the child's own text. The Welsh Orders are wonderful.

G: The parallel to that is the fact that, in writing, there is no attainment target for spelling. Because it's not an issue in Welsh.

E: Is the spelling system in Welsh very different from English?

G: Yes. It is phonetically regular.

H: I have a question. Is an individual who is herself bilingual better able to support bilingualism, as an aspect of children's language use, even where she doesn't share the first language of the children that she is teaching?

E: It depends. If you have a very intelligent child and a monolingual teacher, then it might be OK. But if you have a much less intelligent child, it will be more difficult for the monolingual teacher.

H: A bilingual person understands what it is to move between two or more languages. Is personal experience of that state helpful in attempting to understand and communicate with a child who has a similar experience?

F: I'm sure it is *helpful*, but I would hate to say that it is essential. Because there are all kinds of levels on which I want to communicate with people who have had experiences that I *don't* share – and if I say it is *essential*, and that we can't communicate unless we are alike, then I am cutting myself off from an awful lot of communication and experience. Everything that I can share with people helps. And that is why I reckon we should widen our experience as much as we can. But I would hate to see it said: 'Well you can't do it unless...'.

D: I think this question really is unanswerable in principle, because just as there are people who speak two languages naturally, there are different views about language learning and what it is to speak two languages and so on. At the same time, you might have a regular monolingual speaker of any one particular language, who hasn't been on a language awareness course – and in six weeks they would gain great insight into the problems in having to speak Russian or French, and they could then use that experience: that person would be a better teacher than a natural bilingual person.

G: You are defining bilingual people too narrowly. You have just referred to a monolingual English speaker. However, we touched upon another element of bilingualism earlier today when we referred to which dialect of English speakers have. Practically *everybody* is at least bilingual in the standard and their local speech. They don't have to be separate languages – and that can be enough of an awareness of language problems to make some sense of the people who speak *totally* different languages. But if they don't understand *anything* of that other language, they cannot understand what people say in that other language, so the *crucial* element is actually having someone who understands what the child says. That is the only element which is important to me.

H: You mean a speaker of the language?

G: Someone who *understands* that language adequately enough to respond positively to it.

H: But in the case of these London schools where you might have say...

G: If you have 40 languages, you need 40 people there to speak those languages.

F: Can I have that in writing please?!

G: Yeah. We are talking about bilingualism and how to bring about effective learning in bilingual situations.

H: But it's impossible.

A: If there can be 40 ESL *peripatetic* teachers, why is it impossible?

B: Can you imagine liaising with 40 people?

G: But if you've got 40 children speaking 40 different languages, they need that support.

Summary

The first issue raised concerned the differential treatment by the government of the older indigenous languages (Welsh, Scots-Gaelic and Irish) and the newer minority languages (Panjabi, Bengali, Cantonese, etc.) used in the UK. On the one hand, the government offers financial incentives to resuscitate the Celtic languages. This even extends to linguistic communities which no longer exist – in Belfast and Edinburgh it is now possible for monolingual, English-speaking parents to choose a Gaelic medium school for their children (even though the child's immediate community environment is predominantly English). On the other hand, however, documents such as the Swann and Cox Reports as well as guidelines for Section 11 funding, make it clear that the state is not planning for the maintenance of the community languages spoken by ethnic minorities. 'Linguistic nationalism' was suggested to be the reason why those who have the authority to shape policies favour 'indigenous' languages.

A discussion ensued regarding the actual type of support provided by those Section 11 teachers present – that is, whether they were able to support the child's *first* language (as well as help with their English development). One bilingual support teacher pointed out that, although the *will* to offer this type of provision is often there, on the whole, the *ability* is not. In reply to this, the chair proposed the strategy of teachers working in partnership, suggesting that bilingual staff and monolingual English-speaking mainstream teachers pair up and participate in an intensive two/three week course. During the course, the monolingual teacher should begin to learn the language of some of the pupils.

The Co-ordinator of an English Language Support Service reminded the floor that parental views regarding the use of the mother tongue in school should not be ignored. Indeed, it was recommended that the school language policy should be formulated with these opinions in mind.

A second support teacher pointed out that it would not be fair to set up bilingual learning situations in English and another language – even in schools where 80% of the pupils were speakers of this other language –

because those few children whose first language was neither English nor the other language on offer, would not be catered for in the same way. They would, consequently, be made to feel as though their language were *third*-class. The chair responded by pointing out that a peripatetic teacher could work with these few children to support *their* heritage language in the same way that peripatetic support teachers currently work with isolated bilingual pupils.

Several people were concerned about the low status of bilingual members of staff. One bilingual support teacher wondered whether there might be a link between low status and not being *equally* fluent (yet nevertheless competent) users of two languages. Three of the participants knew of cases where ethnic minority teachers had not been employed because their English was not as good as that of a native-speaker. This situation was compared with the fact that in Wales, teachers who are not very proficient in Welsh *are* given jobs. It was claimed by the Co-ordinator of an English Language Support Service that the problem in England is, therefore, one of racism.

Moving on to the matter of Standard Assessment Tasks, one bilingual support teacher identified the ethos of a school as being a major influence on the performance of their bilingual pupils. For example, her experience of the 1991 SATs was that the bilingual children in one school did very well because the school ethos was 'right', while those in another school did not do very well because of the teachers' attitudes and because of the way they were *taught*.

The implementation of SATs in England was then compared with that in Wales. The floor was informed that in Wales 'SATs should be assessed in the language the child offers'. Commenting on those situations in England where monolingual teachers are not able to assess the under-standing of the pupils, the Director of the Welsh Language Education Development Committee pointed out that such testing is totally incorrect as it *cannot* assess what the child knows. A bilingual support teacher reasoned that bilingual or carefully trained monolingual teachers should therefore carry out SATs.

The final issue was raised by a postgraduate researcher/ESL teacher. Her question was: 'Is an individual who is herself bilingual better able to support bilingualism, as an aspect of children's language use, even where she doesn't share the first language of the children that she is teaching?' One of the support teachers replied that while it may be helpful, being bilingual should not be seen as being *essential*. However, the Director of the Welsh Language Education Development Committee argued that it *is* crucial to have someone who can understand the child's language adequately enough to respond positively to it. In response to protests from the floor about the number of teachers that would be needed to speak *all* the languages of the pupils, the chair pointed out that this could work if managed on a peripatetic basis. Concern was then expressed about liaising with so many teachers! All in all, then, the session produced a great deal of healthy debate and much was learned over the four days as a result of insight into the workings of other Authorities and, indeed, other countries.

8 Promoting Young ESL Children's Written Language Development

LINDY BATES

Young ESL children's use of written language is seen to be influenced by three factors: the way in which written language develops; the attitudes and skills that children bring with them to the writing process; and the effects of the writing context itself. An understanding of these factors can help the teacher to actively promote the young ESL child's ability to express meaning in written language.

Over the last four years I have been researching the ways in which young ESL children's writing develops and how we, as teachers, can promote that development. I became interested in this area after teaching in an English medium school in Malaysia. I was involved in planning and implementing the English syllabus in the Primary section of the school. The teachers with whom I was working had involved the children in doing lots of structured writing but no free writing. They had used comprehension exercises, cloze procedure exercises and multi-choice questions. Story writing only occasionally took place with the aid of a sequence of pictures, sentence openers and a list of vocabulary. Gradually we introduced much more free writing across the curriculum. The children wrote their news, stories and accounts of what they had done in and out of school. In history, geography and science there was more opportunity for the children to write their own notes and accounts rather than always copying from the board.

Gradually, over the course of the next year or so, we found that the children not only became much more confident writers but also became better able to express their meaning orally. This made me wonder whether there was a link between written language development and spoken language development.

When I returned to England I was lucky enough to be able to start a research programme looking at the relationship between the acquisition of literacy skills and the development of spoken language skills. I have been concerned with ESL children during their first two or three years at school when they were learning English for the first time and simultaneously acquiring literacy skills. My attention was focused on children who were able to cope socially in English but were just beginning to use English in its written form.

Spoken language development covers a very broad field. I looked at the uses of spoken language to see where the links might exist between spoken and written language. It seemed to me that decontextualised language was common both to speaking and writing. By decontextualised language I mean language where the words themselves convey the message to the listener. There is nothing in the immediate environment, shared by both speaker and listener, to provide the meaning. For instance, if children want to tell you about things they have done at home, if they want to tell you about their experiences out of school or if they want to tell you a story that exists in their head, then their language will be decontextualised and the words themselves will have to convey the message. In writing also, there is nothing beyond the words on the page to convey the child's message to the reader.

Having identified the area of spoken language which I felt was related to written language, I went into a number of schools and collected samples of the children's written texts. When the children were used to having me around, I also made tapes of small group discussions. The children talked about their homes, their families and their holidays – all the things that I knew nothing about, so they had to make their language clear for me to understand their meaning. I also listened to the children reading in a number of different situations. One of the major findings was that the children who wrote most frequently (writing every day) seemed to be able to express themselves most clearly in spoken language. I am not referring here to accent or to pronunciation, but rather to the children's clear use of language – language that was clear enough for me not to have to wonder what they were talking about or ask for clarification. Another interesting point was that these children were not only able to express their own messages clearly, they were also very good at following a whole conversation and responding to the previous speaker's turn. Sometimes they would collaborate together to tell me something;

sometimes they would clarify or expand on what the previous speaker had said so that I could understand. So they seemed to have good listening skills as well as being able to express meaning clearly.

If one looks at the writing process and at what the children do in decontextualised spoken language, the similarities can be seen. In writing children need to select very carefully the words that they are going to use, they need to put their ideas together in some sort of logical order and they need to express a complete idea. These same demands are made of speakers if they are to make their meaning clear in a decontextualised situation. The listening skills that enable a child to participate effectively in a conversation are also necessary in writing. Young children will usually verbalise what they are going to write, listen to it and then put it down on paper. If they have had to struggle with the spelling, they may then read and re-read their text – both to keep track of what they are saying and also to help them decide what to put next.

If we consider writing within the whole language context, then, it seems clear that we should be regarding writing primarily as a medium for conveying meaning clearly through the language that is used. I am labouring this point somewhat because I am not sure that it is always made clear to children that this is what their writing is for. If a teacher responds to their text by saying: 'You haven't written very much, can you do some more?' or 'That's nice neat writing, well done' or 'You haven't spelt that correctly', children are not going to think that meaning is the most important part of writing.

If we are to work with children to develop their ability to express meaning in writing then we need to understand the developmental patterns in writing; we need to understand what children bring with them to the writing process and also the effects of the writing context on the language that children use. I shall be looking at each of these three areas below.

The Developmental Patterns in Writing

Structure

I will start by discussing the developmental patterns in children's writing. During my research I looked both at ESL children's writing and also at the writing of their E1L peers. I did this because it is important to establish the target language. I will provide texts written by both groups to illustrate the ways in which texts written by this age group (5–8 year olds) can develop.

Texts develop in a number of different ways and I will start by talking about the ways in which ideas are linked together throughout a text – the structure of the text. If we look at the following three clauses:

It is a nice day
The children are going out
I have a headache

It is not at all clear how or if the three ideas are linked. The children may be going out because it is a nice day, or because the author has a headache. Equally, the children could be going out but the author cannot, because she has a headache. The links must be made explicitly in order to make the meaning clear. Ideas can be linked through the use of conjunctions: *and, but, then, because* and *so; through the use of subordination: when it was dark I went to bed;* or through ellipsis: *the bear went and got into bed.* Two clauses are run together here because in the second clause the child has left out the subject.

We will now consider how these features develop. When young children begin writing they use unlinked clauses. For example, Mary-Anne has written down a number of statements which are apparently unconnected:

'I am a girl I am six I like to play' (6 year old Filippino speaker)

Later, clauses are linked with the conjunction 'and' as in Lyanne's text:

'I like to go swimming in my back garden with my mummy and my daddy and my sister **and** *I like it* **and** *I can swim'* (5 year old English speaker).

Surjit's ideas are linked with 'and' but she has also made use of a subordinate when clause. These are the first of the subordinate clauses to appear. Surjit had brought in her favourite Christmas card and decided to write a story about it:

'Once upon a time the snowman and the bear were friends **and** *the bear wanted to kiss her* **and when** *he did her lips melted* **and** *he had to make her new lips with the snow* **and** *the snow bear said thank you* **and** *the bear gave the flower to the bear'* (7 year old Panjabi speaker).

The full range of conjunctions gradually appears and makes the meaning very much clearer, as in Lorna's account of a stormy night:

'There was a storm on Saturday night. It was very windy. I woke up in the middle of the storm. I was in my bed **and** *watched the storm for a little while.* **Then** *I went out of my bedroom to tell my Mum* **but** *she was already coming out of her bedroom with Chris* **because** *Chris was frightened of the thunder.'* (6 year old English speaker).

Note how Lorna has used all the different types of conjunction to make her meaning clear. She has also begun to separate her text into sentences.

Debbie, who was a year older, not only uses the full range of conjunctions but also makes use of subordination to structure her text:

> '*Once upon a time there was a little owl* **who** *was looking for a husband,* **when** *she saw two little owls getting married.* **Then** *the little owl,* **whose** *name was Ratty had an idea "Push off Fatso this is my husband" said Ratty.....*'

Amongst the ESL children in the study, there was very little use of sentence structure or of subordination. They tended to make the greatest use of '*and*' and '*and then*' to link their ideas.

To summarise, then, young children seem to make use of structural devices in the following order. First they use unlinked clauses, and then clauses linked with '*and*'. This is followed by a growing use of the full range of conjunctions together with an emergence of '*when*' clauses. Finally, young children begin to organise their ideas into sentences and use an increasing amount of subordination.

Story development

We will now discuss story development – how ideas are developed throughout a text. Stories seem to develop in two different ways. Young children make an increasing use of the elements of story structure. They also move from the concrete and personal towards the imaginary. I found that this was very marked amongst the ESL children. They seemed to find it easier to write about things which were very personal or to put *themselves* into a story, rather than writing about something which was imaginary.

Story structure does come up in the National Curriculum but what is actually meant is not made quite as clear as I would like to see it. The important point is that each part of the story develops from the part that has come before. It develops as follows:

(i)   introduction of the setting (perhaps '*Once upon a time*' or '*One day*')
(ii) introduction of the characters ('*There was a ...*')
(iii) an initiating event (something which gets the story going)
(iv) the development of the plot, which leads on from the initiating event
(v)   the resolution, which sorts out the exciting part, and
(vi) the conclusion ('*they lived happily ever after*' or even just '*the end*').

If we look again at Surjit's story we can see how she has used a full story structure:

Introduction of setting	*'Once upon a time*
Introduction of characters	*the snowman and the bear were friends*
Initiating event	*and the bear wanted to kiss her*
Development of the plot	*and when he did her lips melted and he had to make her new lips with the snow*
Resolution	*and the snow bear said thank you and the bear gave the flower to the bear*
Conclusion	*the end'*

We will now examine some narrative texts in terms of their story structure and the effects of being able to relate the subject matter to the child's own experience. The following two texts were both written by Jason, a 6 year old Panjabi speaker:

'A spider changed into spiderman and he caught someone in a web'

Jason's class had been watching a television programme featuring a spider which, I think, must have blown away in the wind. The teacher asked the children to write a story about where the spider might have blown. Jason seems to have encapsulated a good story idea but there is no development beyond the two events. In his second story, Jason has taken his ideas further. The class had been reading the story of Noah. They knew it very well and had been drawing pictures of the Ark. On this occasion the teacher had suggested that they write a story about what they would have done on the Ark. In Jason's text, we can see the effect of the personal element which seems to be important in the early stages of story writing:

'God made the flood and I took all the animals inside they were hungry they wanted to jump out I locked them up'

This time Jason has an initiating event and much more development of the plot. It is worth noting here how much more explicit his meaning would have been if he had used a wider range of conjunctions. For instance, he could have written:

'...they were hungry **so** *they wanted to jump out* **but** *I locked them up'*.

Here is another spider story. The previous night, Rosie's aunt had been burgled. Note how Rosie has been able to make use of this personal experience in her text:

'A spider went in someone's cupboard and someone's jewellery was stolen and the lady was angry and the lady phoned policeman and the policeman got him then lady saw the spider and she scream her head off and the spider went home' (6 year old Panjabi speaker).

Comparing the E1L texts with the ESL children's writing, it seemed that story telling was the natural genre of the E1L children at this stage. They turned whatever they were asked to write about into a story. However, this was not so for the ESL children with whom I was working. There seems to be a need for these children to really know and understand the topic before they use the narrative form. The language used by the teacher is also important and I will return to this point later.

I will now illustrate the need to understand a topic. In one school, a travelling theatre had enacted the story of the first steam engines and the children were later asked to write about the theatre group's visit. In another school a man had brought four owls to the school and had talked about their feeding and breeding habits. Again, the children were asked to write about the visit. All the E1L children wrote a story about owls while the ESL children wrote accounts of the theatre's visit. If we look briefly at the opening stages of some of the children's texts, the differences are obvious. Rosemary (a 7 year old E1L speaker) began:

'One day there lived a family of owls. One day they decided to go for a fly. First the mother owl said I think we should teach our owlets to fly.....'

Paul (a 7 year old Panjabi speaker) wrote:

'We had a play and they had a horse.....'

Shamela (a 7 year old Urdu speaker) began in a similar way:

'Yesterday afternoon we saw a play and there was a girl called Jo and she showed us a witch face.....'

It appeared that the ESL children had found it difficult to follow the play and so were not in a position to turn what they had seen into a story. Instead they wrote accounts of the afternoon, focusing on the actual events rather than the story. This highlights the fact that story writing needs to be based on material that the children really know and understand.

Elaboration

I now wish to turn to the next area of development: elaboration. Kiran has given us two facts in her writing:

'*I went to the shops and I have a look round*' (7 year old Panjabi speaker)
She has provided no extra details. On the other hand, Charlene (a 5 year
old English speaker), who has also given us two facts, has provided
many more details:

> '*I went to the beach and me and my sister went in the sea and we went in the
> sea because me and my sister got all sandy feet and so we paddled our feet
> and it was fun*'

Charlene has given an explanation of why they went in the sea. There is also
some description (it was *sandy*), and an evaluative comment (*it was fun*).

Elaboration makes use of description, evaluation, explanation and
direct or reported speech. All of these features can be used to create
elaborated narratives rather than core narratives. The ESL children were
very able at expressing their meaning in core narratives. Elaboration,
however, provides a way of developing written or spoken language – of
making meaning more detailed.

It seems that children firstly make use of description. Jason (a 6 year
old Panjabi speaker) wrote about playing with his brother:

> '*I played cars with my brother and he had a police car and my one was a
> yellow truck*'

He has told us that his brother's car was *a police car* and his was *a yellow
truck*. Emily (a 5 year old English speaker) has gone further:

> '*I have a goldfish and her name is Ouisy she has lots of fish food and it cost
> lots of money. and one day my brother spilt all of the gold fish food and I was
> cross*'

Emily was writing about her pets. We know she has a goldfish and are
told what the goldfish's name is. She then goes on to describe how much
food the goldfish has, how expensive it is and how she felt one day when
her brother spilt all this expensive food. Emily has used description and
evaluation, and there is a hint of explanation for surely she is cross with
her brother because the food is so expensive. Explanations often begin in
this way – by being implicit rather than explicit.

Let us examine two more stories. Ravinder (a 6 year old Panjabi
speaker) has written about a bear:

> '*Once a little bear lived in London zoo the owner got the panda bear and let
> him go the panda bear saw another zoo he went inside and the guards got
> him and put him in the kavi the end*'

Danielle, (a 6 year old English speaker) has written about a magic island:

> *'One day a littel boy went to climb a Island it was a magic Island. The littel Boy did not no it was a magic Island the boy went up and up he sleput and he fall done the Island. He fall injured on the floor. The people colde a ambulance. The ambulance came has qweik has they code and they toc hem to hospital. And the people code hes mum and DaD hes mum and DaD went to the hospital. Hes mum was crying* (because their son had broken his leg).'

Ravinder has written a clear and well developed narrative but he has only used one item of description: *'little'*. The reader is left with lots of questions. Why did the owner let the bear go? Why did he go to another zoo? Was he happy in his cave? Danielle, on the other hand, has provided her readers with far more detail. We know that the boy is *'little'*, and that the island is *'magic'*. The boy fell *'injured'* and the ambulance came *'as quick as it could'*. Like Emily, Danielle has hinted that something happened to the boy because the island was magic – it looks as though she wanted to write that the boy's mother was crying because the boy was injured. This extra information was added to the text by the teacher. Although Danielle has not quite used speech, she refers to the people calling for the ambulance and sending for the boy's parents.

The ESL children do all seem to start elaborating their texts by using description, and in their personal writing they use evaluation. They appear to use very little explanation. Only about 30% of the children I studied used explanation, as opposed to 100% of the E1L children. During the time I was working with these children, I also noticed that they asked very few questions as well as giving very few explanations. Their teachers had noticed this too. Perhaps the children felt that it was inappropriate in some way to ask questions or to proffer explanations. However, I did find that during the group discussions, if I asked a *'why'* question, the children would respond with an explicit *'because'* answer.

Before leaving this area, I would like to share one delightful story with you, which was written almost entirely through reported speech by Aliya (a 7 year old Urdu speaker):

> *'The Lazy Old Bear*
> *Once upon a time a Bear was going by untell he met his freid called Lazy Bear*
> *Wat are you doing lazy Bear ast his freid*
> *Im jast laying*
> *well im glad thet Im not*

way said lazy Bear
becomes his freid said
I don't cear said lazy Bear and soon they begen to have a faiut and they ageud and
then lazy Bears Mum camed and said lave my son alon
way said hes freid
do whte my mummy says said Lazy Bear
okay then my freid I well lave you alon and they lave happly avre afta The End.'

Aliya seems to have captured just the type of conversation that might go on in the school playground. Young children seem to be incredibly adept at using speech in their stories. They appear to use it to home in on the details that they want to slow down and highlight, whereas older children seem to use extended conversations that add little to the main part of the narrative:

> *'Is it time to get up yet? I said. Yes said Mum. So I got up and said Is it time for breakfast?'*

To summarise, then, children begin by using descriptive terms, perhaps relating to size, colour or number. They then add their own evaluative comments. The use of speech and explanation appear as their texts develop further.

Reference uses

We turn now to reference. *Endophoric reference* refers to pronouns and the definite article which can be understood from within the text itself. For example:

> *'One day a boy called Robson was going to make a cake and he went to the kitchen.'*

The reader knows exactly who '*he*' is because Robson has already been mentioned.

> *'There was once a reindeer and* **he** *had no home'*

Again we know who '*he*' is in the above sentence because the reindeer has already been mentioned.

> *'A dog chased a cat.* **The** *dog caught* **the** *cat.'*

Here we understand the use of the definite article because a cat and a dog have already been introduced.

Exophoric reference refers to pronouns and the definite article which can only be understood by looking outside the text. For example, if a child writes a bare statement·such as:

'*He is chasing the cat*'

we have no idea who '*he*' is without going outside the text to look, for instance, at the child's drawing. Within written language, reference items therefore need to be endophoric for the meaning to be clear. Within decontextualised speech, again, reference items need to be endophoric for the meaning to be clear to the listener.

The same pattern of use occurs within both E1L and ESL writing. Helen's texts illustrate what tends to happen:

'**The** *trains had a race and Rocket won the race Jo cam back and No one was they and* **the** *horse came to say where is Puffing Billy*.'

We do not know to which trains Helen is referring and we do not know which horse she means. She has used exophoric reference. In Helen's own story, however, the reference items are clear.

'*Once upon a time there was a kind wolf* **He** *lived in a cave then a big bad wolf* **the** *bad wolf found* **the** *kind cave bad wolf had a fight* **the** *good wolf won and lived happily ever after*'

Helen has correctly used the indefinite article for the first mention, and only then has she used the definite article. The children seem to use endophoric reference when they are writing about something the reader has not shared with them. However, when they are writing about something which the reader has shared with them, they use exophoric reference. This is also the case in the writing of E1L children. It is noticeable amongst older children when they write about science experiments which they have done with the teacher, for example.

So the developmental pattern to be found shows firstly the use of endophoric reference when the child is writing something personal or a story where the teacher/reader has not shared the same frame of reference. Only later does the child manage to use endophoric reference when writing about things which the teacher/reader does already know about.

Vocabulary

The final area of development I wish to discuss is that of vocabulary. There were three areas of development that I found amongst the E1L children and yet seldom found amongst the ESL group. Children seem to start off by using a simple basic vocabulary. The E1L children then went on to express what I have called 'different shades of meaning'. Instead of writing *'went'*, for example, they were able to use more differentiated terms such as *'ran'*, *'walked'*, *'limped'* and so on. They also made use of topic specific vocabulary. Again, the ESL children were very good at being able to put across their meaning using the vocabulary that they did have, but they lacked the depth of vocabulary which their E1L peers had. Kamaljit, for instance, went to the circus and wrote *'the people are very funny'* because she did not know the word for 'clowns'. There is a need to enable the ESL children to build up both topic specific terms and also a range of words to provide different shades of meaning.

Having now looked at five areas of development in young children's writing (structure, story development, elaboration, reference and vocabulary), I now wish to consider what the children bring with them to the writing process. We can then discuss teaching strategies to promote language development.

The Writing Process

First and foremost, when I was talking with the children, it was obvious that they had a very good knowledge of the principles of discourse – as one would expect. Even though they were communicating within the constraints of a second or even a third language, they knew perfectly well how they were required to behave within a conversational context. If a question was asked, they had to give an answer; if one speaker said something, the next contribution had to be appropriate; if they were going to introduce a topic, they had to make it quite clear what they were talking about. We have all had the experience of children who have put their hands up and started: *'You know, you know Miss, my big brother'* – when you have indicated that you do know of their big brother, they can then continue to tell you what they wanted to say. It is very important, if we are to consider writing as expressing meaning, that we respond to children's texts in the same way that we respond to speech. In speech children know whether they have made their meaning clear because the listener will either be nodding or asking for clarification if they need it. When children are writing, there is a tendency to not always do this – indeed, there isn't always time. And yet, it is only by responding to meaning and operating within an area that children understand, that they can develop or adapt their language to make their meaning clearer. I therefore believe that one of the major teaching strategies should be to interact with individual children during the writing process, and to respond to their meaning – if it is possible to go round the classroom whilst they are writing. The teacher can then ask for further details, or for the child's opinions or feelings, or for explanations. If we look back at elaboration, I would suggest that interaction during the writing process is the best way in which it can be encouraged.

One of the other major observations that I made was that children's experience of reading affects their use of language when they are writing. It is not the stories which have been heard that are so important. Two parallel classes were taking part in the research, which heard the same stories during the school day. One class, however, was very much better at reading, and the children also used many more structural devices in their writing, such as conjunctions, subordinate clauses and sentence structure. The child's reading experience also seems to affect the use of verb tenses. In Malaysia I was working with children who were reading Ladybird books. The early stages of Ladybird make exclusive use of the present tense. It was very noticeable that the children who only read Ladybird books used present tense in their own writing, whereas children with a wider experience of books used a range of tenses.

Three texts illustrate this point. Salha (a 7 year old Arabic speaker), who had been reading Ladybird, wrote:

'the witch **hates** the children and the children **are** afraid the witch **changes** the children into a frog'

Joanne (a 6 year old Cantonese speaker), who had also been reading Ladybird, began her story:

'the witch **get** her broomstick to **go** up, she go up to see Charlie because she **wants** to talk to Charlie please can you help me Charlie **says** I can help you . . . . .'

In contrast, Lip Jin (a 5 year old Cantonese speaker), who had read a wide range of books, wrote:

'I **looked** out of the window and I **saw** a witch, she **has** a black hat and she **has** a broomstick and her magic wand and she **had** a kind face.'

It has also been found that children reading basic readers tend to use a very disjointed writing style reflecting the style of the readers. If the experience of their own reading materials affects the language used by children in this way, in order to develop structure in writing we should perhaps consider modelling structures in children's reading materials. Writing stories for the children to read, carefully selecting books or even writing letters to the children could provide opportunities to model appropriate structural items.

Another important factor is the child's degree of independence in writing. If writing is to be a way of developing children's use of language, then we want them to be able to develop their ideas and express their meaning as fully as they can in writing. If children are dependent upon the teacher to provide the words they need, the writing process will be continuously interrupted, or they will rely upon the limited vocabulary that they know how to spell. Let us consider two children in a Year 1 class. Rumi (a 6 year old Bengali speaker) had not got going on developmental spelling at all, and she only used those words she could find around the classroom or which she was certain she knew:

> '*I went to the shops*'.

For weeks Rumi wrote sentences like '*I went to the shop*' or '*I saw a dog*'. These were not events which had necessarily happened, but Rumi felt secure in using those particular words. Note the difference in language between Rumi's writing and Ricky's:

> '*I bord my fres skip I went hom to sa dad I wut a skip rop I sed dad I wut a skip rop theen I can pla wiv my fres theen I can pla evda wiv my udwis I ha to pla wiv my fres skip rop*'
> (I borrowed my friend's skipping rope I went home to say Dad I want a skipping rope then I can play with my friends then I can play everyday with my friends otherwise I have to play with my friend's skipping rope).

Ricky did not have to interrupt himself to go to the teacher, as he had enough knowledge of letter names and sounds to put all his ideas down on paper. Developmental writing and the use of invented spelling when the standard form is not known, does seem to liberate children to express their meaning as fully as possible.

However, encouraging the children to become independent writers is not always as straightforward as it may sound. Why, for instance, did Ricky become an independent writer while Rumi relied for so long on the few words she could see or remember?

As I observed more children it became clear that children can come into school with quite different ideas as to what writing is all about. Writing can be seen as a copying exercise, copying from a book or an adult model to make a neat display. It can be seen as using letters or symbols to make a message. It can be using letter names or letter sounds to represent speech sounds, or children may even feel that writing is something that they cannot do. During the last four years I have come across all of these attitudes amongst children in their first year or two at school.

The attitude that writing meant copying was the one of which I was most aware, and it was an attitude that had removed any sense of meaning from the writing process. Some of the children were learning to form their letters at home or at the gurdwara, mosque or community school. The approach seemed to be that children must be able to form all the letters correctly before they could start writing words. To experiment with those letters to convey meaning would have been quite inappropriate. I spent a year visiting one particular Year 1 class in which there were several children who seemed to equate writing with copying (one of whom was Rumi). They would spend hours copying any sample of writing they could find. Sometimes it would be a piece of their teacher's writing; sometimes it would be a book. They would complete a page of painstaking writing and then proudly present it for inspection. If we ever asked what the text said, they would be very surprised that we thought it should have meaning. These children did not seem to have the idea that they could make meaning with their writing. Unless one can explicitly show the children that it is appropriate for them to make meaning with their own writing, development may be very slow. In this particular class, it was activities such as sending Christmas cards and writing letters to their mothers for Mothering Sunday that suddenly opened up the possibilities of meaningful writing for the children.

In a study which I carried out to look at the different concepts ESL and E1L children might have about writing, I had the help of a bilingual speaker so that all the instructions were given to the ESL children in their preferred language. Amongst other things we asked the children, who were aged between 4.9 and 5.10 years, to write a letter to their mothers and post them in a postbox. The differences between the two groups were interesting. Most of the E1L children completed a page of play writing, using varied displays of the letters that they knew, or even using scribble writing. Some of the ESL children wrote as much of the alphabet as they knew and even included numbers from 1 to 10. There was a vast difference in the starting points of these two groups of children. The ESL children had a greater knowledge of the actual letter formations and they were aware of the differences between English writing and the script of their mother tongue. The E1L children, on the other hand, were more aware of what they could do with the letters that they did know. This clearly has implications for encouraging developmental writing.

I now wish to examine young children's ability to edit their written text – to respond critically to their own writing. There are children who are able to read through, listen to what they have written, and then change a word or two, or even more. I wish to present the first evidence we had in the Year 1 class that young children were capable of quite major editing. On the whole, the class teacher did not expect the children to edit because she felt that, after all the effort they had put into producing a piece of writing at this early stage, they would not want to continue working on the same text. On this occasion, however, Nitesh (a 6 year old Panjabi speaker) had first told his story to the teacher and then went away to write it. When he had finished and read it through to his teacher, she commented that he had originally told her a bit more. Nitesh was able to look at his text, see what was missing and then rewrite it so that his meaning would be clear to his reader:

1st Draft

'ter wus a man and the mans nam wus suniy and ter wus a robr and the robr got in prisan and suniy horse kam bak'

(There was a man and the man's name was Sunny and there was a robber and the robber got in prison and Sunny's horse came back).

2nd Draft

'ter was a man and the mans nam was Suney and suney had a horse and ter wus a robr and the robr got the horse and the man rag the pulles and the robr got in prisn'.

This ability to re-read critically with an awareness of the reader's needs obviously helps children to develop their texts and make their meaning clearer.

Motivation

Finally in this section concerning what children bring with them to the writing process, I wish to raise the issue of motivation – the children's level of involvement with their own writing. In the Year 1 class I visited, the children were explicitly taught how to generate their own writing using their growing knowledge of the letter names and sounds. They also had access to vocabulary in wall displays and on word cards. The teacher and I both felt that the children had the necessary skills to write independently and yet they were still restricting themselves to 'I saw' or 'I went' texts. Gradually, however, each child began to take off. Examining the texts below, it is clear that they were writing about things which were really personal and meaningful to them. It was this intensely personal involvement which seemed to motivate children to use the skills they already possessed.

Ricky had just had his birthday party:

'Ahmed like Ricky and Shane like Ricky Ahmed came to Ricky partiy and went my partiy I plad tgev'

Reena had watched the film of Raymond Briggs' Snowman. She wrote:

'I vot the snumn to come to my put AnD i vot the mum to m a k' (I want the snowman to come to my party and I want Mum to make a cake).

Rumi wrote her letter to her mother for Mothering Sunday:

'to mummy I like my mummy my mummy gave me chip love from Rumi'
In each case, the children had worked alone to produce their texts and from then on their writing began to really develop.

This personal involvement seems to be important all the way through primary school. I worked with a 9 year old Bengali speaker who had not done any free writing, although, as far as we knew, he had been in an English medium school since the age of five. During the first session I asked Toymur about his family and his home – both in England and in Bangladesh. I had made some word cards, and as Toymur gave me information, I picked out the words so that he could write it down. Before long, Toymur had taken over the task of choosing the cards and of providing the information. Over the next few weeks, Toymur began spontaneously and independently to write his own news in the classroom. It was, I believe, the personal involvement that prompted Toymur to begin to write for himself.

So far, then, we have looked at the ways in which young children's writing develops. We have looked at what children bring with them to the writing process in terms of attitude and motivation. I now wish to look at the effects of the writing context itself upon the language used by the child.

The Writing Context

I found that the language used by the teacher in introducing a topic can influence what a child will write. I carried out a study in which 6–8 year old children were asked, amongst other things, to choose a Christmas card from a wide selection and to *'write a story* **about** *the picture'*. Emma (a 7 year old Spanish speaker) knew that she had to write a story so she started with a traditional story opener and then, because she had been asked to write about the card, she proceeded to describe it:

'One day there was two girls and a Christmas tree is next to the girl in the red and I like the blue curtains and the christmas pudding it is white and

brown and the green shoes are plane and she got a teddy bear. Next to her the
bear has brown feet the tree has little people on it.'

You could almost draw the card from what Emma wrote. This happened with a number of the ESL children. They seemed to be very sensitive to the detail of what was said to them by the teacher. Thinking back to the travelling theatre where the ESL children wrote accounts rather than stories, the teacher had again suggested that the children write **about** the theatre's visit to the school.

Whilst teaching in the classroom, a teacher trainer, Ann Robinson, found that her E1L children were also very influenced by what she said before they began writing. Rather than follow their own train of thoughts, they tended to faithfully reproduce what she had suggested. Ann Robinson then collected a number of objects, put them into a box and left a notice suggesting that the objects in the box were sad because they had no story to belong to. Following this, the children's narrative writing developed enormously as they pursued their own ideas. One could do the same with pictures, suggesting that children put the pictures into a story. Giving children the opportunity to follow their own train of thought and not over-structuring their writing is very important. For instance, when we gave children a sequence of pictures to write a story, thus providing a tight structure for their writing, we found that their texts lacked development and did not contain many elements of story structure. Stories written by the same children without any structuring were far more developed.

I also found that if children wrote stories after a great deal of classroom discussion, there was a tendency for them to omit the introduction of the setting and characters. They tended to plunge straight into the action, presumably because they felt that they were continuing with a topic already understood by the teacher. There is a need, perhaps, to identify an external audience who knows nothing about the topic so that children will need to introduce their story clearly. This links back to the use of endophoric and exophoric reference. The child's use of endophoric reference is affected by whether or not the teacher already knows about the writing topic. Again, the use of an external audience could be helpful.

Teaching Strategies

I would now like to draw together all the above by outlining some teaching strategies to develop the child's expression of meaning in writing. We can look again at the five areas of development in the light of what children bring with them to the writing process and the effects of the writing context.

Story development can be encouraged in many different ways. I would like to draw attention here to helping the children to become aware of the structure of stories. Stories can be talked about in terms of where the story is set, who is in it, what is going to happen, and how it might end. I have suggested that children need to understand a topic fully before they can write a story about it, and that the personal involvement is very important. The use of known stories as a loose structure can be useful, particularly if children can put themselves into the story. The children's knowledge of the principles of discourse means that they will be conscious of the needs of a reader who does not share their frame of reference. The use of an external audience could therefore be helpful. The way in which we introduce story topics can also be important. As children gain more confidence as writers, plenty of opportunity could be provided for them to develop their own stories.

The use of an increasing range of structural devices could be encouraged through the careful choice of reading material. I have suggested that it is probable that children's own reading material influences their own written language.

The use of elaboration can be encouraged through interacting with the child during the writing process, responding first and foremost to the child's meaning. Again, it is the child's awareness of the need to clarify one's meaning, to provide extra information in spoken language, which should be built on here. Also, by listening to children's texts and commenting on them, we may encourage children to listen to their own texts and critically assess what they have written.

The child's use of endophoric reference can be encouraged through the use of an external audience and also through asking for clarification wherever the meaning is not clear. There is obviously a need to provide frequent opportunities for ESL children to develop their vocabulary. I have suggested that the children will need topic specific vocabulary and vocabulary to express different shades of meaning.

Finally, I hope that I have highlighted the need to be aware of children's own attitudes towards writing, their views on what is appropriate and their feeling of personal involvement in the writing process.

9 Old Sounds and New Sounds: Bilinguals Learning ESL

MAHENDRA K. VERMA and SALLY FIRTH

The research project 'Working with Bilingual Children' has, amongst other things, been studying the cognitive and linguistic development of potential bilinguals in British primary schools. This paper deals with the acquisition of spoken English as a second language by children whose mother tongue is Panjabi or Urdu. Two groups of children are considered, one group in West Yorkshire and the other in Edinburgh. We found that the spoken English of these children displayed assimilation towards the regional accent of their monolingual English-speaking peers as well as preserving their ethnic identity through the accent of English spoken by South Asian adults. We conclude by commenting on the implications this has for bilingual children with respect to the National Curriculum.

Introduction

While there has been a significant amount of research on the phonology (sound system) of the non-native English spoken in the Indian subcontinent (see, for example, Bansal, 1969, 1983; Barron, 1961a, 1961b; Pandit, 1964; Rao, 1961; Sethi, 1978, 1979, 1980; Varma, 1957; Wells, 1982b), the English phonology of second/third generation children born *in Britain* has not received the same attention. Apart from the work by Agnihotri (1979) concerning Panjabi-speaking Sikh children in Leeds, there are only very brief generalisations of 'pronunciation difficulties' to be found within works encompassing a much wider field of bilingual classroom research. For example, in Tough (1985: 76), the coverage of phonological acquisition by such children amounts to one sentence. One of the aims of our study, then, was to establish the English phonological system acquired by the children/grandchildren of South Asian migrants in Britain.

Methodology

The actual data collected for detailed investigation comprises recordings of 17 children whose mother tongue is Mirpuri Panjabi or Urdu. The children attend primary schools in West Yorkshire (one school in Batley and one in Dewsbury) and in Edinburgh (one school in the city centre and one in Leith). Nine of the children (aged 5) were in the reception class, and will have had little exposure to English up to their entry into this class. The other eight were of the age at which they undergo national testing (aged 7 in England, and 8 in Scotland). Table 9.1 gives further details of the background of the children.

Table 9.1 Details of the subjects

No. of subjects	Age	Sex	Mother tongue	Area
6	5 yrs	4♂ 2♀	Panjabi/Urdu	West Yorkshire
4	7 yrs	2♂ 2♀	Panjabi/Urdu	West Yorkshire
3	5 yrs	0♂ 3♀	Panjabi/Urdu	Edinburgh
4	8 yrs	2♂ 2♀	Panjabi/Urdu	Edinburgh

Each child was recorded at regular intervals throughout the course of a year in order to follow their linguistic progress. The recordings are of natural connected speech: conversations between the researcher and the children (both individually and in groups), and between the children and their peers (both monolingual and bilingual).

We set out to address the following question: *What are the motivating factors which cause an ESOL* (English for speakers of other languages) *learner to adopt one realisation over a number of competing alternatives?* A contrastive analysis of learners exposed to phonologically *divergent* varieties of British English enabled us to produce more accurate (and predictive) answers to this. The significance of observing within more than one dialect region is clear from the fieldworker's report on the use of the definite article by learners in both groups, for example. During Firth's research on the Yorkshire children whose mother tongues were Panjabi/Urdu, she observed that they frequently omitted the definite article and wondered whether this might be due to influence from the local vernacular. For example, S.A. (aged 7, from Dewsbury, West Yorkshire) produced the utterance: 'Then I went to doctor's'. From the context it is apparent that the reference attached to *doctor's* is definite and as such in

Standard English it would be preceded by the definite article *the*. In Yorkshire dialect, however, in phrases such as *to the doctor's, the* is frequently reduced to a glottal stop. It seemed quite probable at this juncture that S.A. had either not perceived or could not as yet produce the required glottal stop. However, during Firth's research in Scotland, she noted that the Edinburgh learners *also* failed to produce definite articles in contexts where they would be required by native English speakers. Since the reduction of *the* to a glottal stop is not a Scottish characteristic, the phenomenon did not, after all, seem to be related to a Yorkshire influence. In fact, the uniform pattern exhibited by both groups is more likely to be the result of inappropriate transfer from the mother tongue – Panjabi and Urdu do not have equivalents for the English definite article and express determiner reference by other means, including ø. Had this research project been limited to ESOL learners of *Yorkshire* English, it would in this case have given a false result and it is not difficult to envisage such inappropriate conclusions being drawn about aspects of the children's phonological acquisition.

The Acquisitional Environment

The acquisitional environment of English for speakers of other languages differs from those which have normally been the focus of research in the field of language acquisition in Britain. The richness and diversity of the input data, the educational and societal target models of English, and the motivation and pressures to acquire and sustain competence in the mother tongue make language-learning processes for these minority children in British primary schools different from their peers who have English as their mother tongue. In order to understand and make observations on the developing phonological system of these bilingual or potentially bilingual children, we must examine their 'interlanguage' against the background of this sociolinguistic bilingual repertoire and we must do so in terms of both 'transfer' and 'developmental' constructs. In order to appreciate the role of 'transfer', one must consider the languages that form part of the children's experience, as well as the *roles* of those languages (see Figure 9.1). The developmental aspect is closely linked with educational intervention (especially in the context of the requirements of the National Curriculum (compulsory in England and Wales) and the 5–14 programme (compulsory in Scotland)), and particularly with the roles played by bilingual support and mainstream teachers.

It should be noted that our subjects attend schools where a large proportion of the children do not speak English on entering school. In

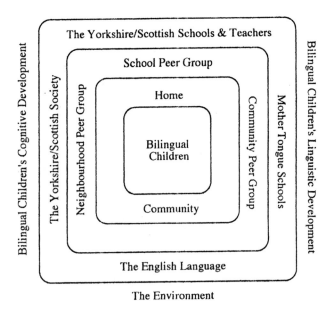

Figure 9.1 Bilingual children in Britain

some schools, over 80% of the pupils have a mother tongue other than English. The rate of acquisition of English, including its phonology, might therefore not be as accelerated as one might expect, because their exposure to English in the classroom will be more limited than has been the case for the subjects of other studies in the field of second language acquisition. Indeed, for *some* of our subjects, the sole providers of spoken English appear to be their class teacher, a handful of monolingual English-speaking peers in their class, and the Teenage Mutant Hero Turtles (from whom most of our subjects seem to receive regular input)!

The Influence of Various Sound Systems

The *sound system* of a language can be thought of as the set of sounds used in a language. Each language has a different sound system. For instance, German does not have /w/ in its sound system. For this reason, a German speaking English may replace /w/ with [v] and pronounce words such as *we* and *wait* as 've' and 'vait'. Similarly, Received Pronunciation (RP, often known as 'BBC English') does not have the sound which occurs at the end of the German surname 'Bach' (phonetically transcribed as /bax/) – thus, most RP speakers pronounce this name in the same way that they pronounce 'bark'.

It is not only different *languages* which have different sound systems: different varieties of the same language are also made up of different repertoires of sounds. The sound systems of Yorkshire English, Scottish English and RP are all different from each other. This can be illustrated by just one example – the realisation of words containing sounds spelled with the letter 'u'. Yorkshire English does not have the sound used by both RP speakers and speakers of Scottish English when they say *bus*. Furthermore, Scottish English does not have the sound used by both RP speakers and speakers of Yorkshire English when they say *put*.

Due to the delayed opportunity to acquire English, then, the spoken English of the children in our study will inevitably contain *interference* from the different sound system of their first language – Panjabi or Urdu. Moreover, the 17 children under consideration are exposed to two quite different varieties of English – both of which are different again from RP, the variety of English which several studies have assumed to be the target language of *all* ESOL learners. This means that the children's spoken English will also be influenced by the sound system of the variety of English spoken where they are growing up.

We will now discuss tokens in our data of these kinds of influence – firstly dealing with the influence from the children's first language, and secondly from the English of their local environment. The following abbreviations will be used:

P/U: Panjabi/Urdu   SE: Scottish (Edinburgh) English

RP: Received Pronunciation (BBC)   YE: (West) Yorkshire English

The Influence of Panjabi/Urdu

Apart from five sounds, Panjabi and Urdu are made up of the same sound system. The only difference is that Urdu has the sounds /bh/, /dh/, /jh/, /ḍh/, and /gh/, while Panjabi does not. As these five sounds never occurred in the English speech of any of the 17 children with whom we worked, we do not need to discuss the influence of the Panjabi sound system separately from the influence of the Urdu sound system. Throughout the rest of this paper, we will therefore be referring to 'Panjabi/Urdu' (P/U) rather than Panjabi *and/or* Urdu.

Vowels

RP has 20 vowels in its sound system. These vowels are listed in Table 9.2.

Table 9.2 The vowels of RP

	IPA symbol	Example word	Is it in the P/U sound system?
1	i	these	Yes
2	ɪ	bid	Yes
3	ɛ	bed	No
4	a	bad	No
5	ɑ	card	Yes
6	ɒ	hot	No
7	ɔ	horse	Yes
8	ʊ	book	Yes
9	u	rule	Yes
10	ʌ	bus	No
11	ɜ	bird	No
12	ə	<u>a</u>ccount	Yes
13	eɪ	gate	No
14	oʊ	home	No
15	aɪ	bite	No
16	aʊ	house	No
17	ɒɪ	boil	No
18	ɪə	cheer	No
19	ɛə	air	No
20	ʊə	cure	No

As one might expect, however, the number of vowels varies between one variety of English and another. Despite this, the number of vowels in both YE and SE is greater than the number in P/U – YE has 18 vowels in its sound system (see Gimson, 1980: 101–46, or Wells, 1982a: 351–65 for details) and SE has 15 vowels (see Gimson, 1980: 101–46; Wells, 1982a: 399–408, or Hawkins, 1984: 239 for details). Since there are only 10 vowels in P/U, the children are therefore faced with the task of learning several new vowels during their acquisition of English.

There seem to be relatively few sounds in the speech of our subjects which are influenced by P/U vowels. This is probably due to the fact that there are fewer vowels in their mother tongue repertoire to cause interference. Only two vowels were pronounced in a way which we could ascribe to influence from P/U. These were vowel numbers 11 and 18 from Table 9.2. Thus, the vowel in the words *shirt* and (fire)*works* was produced too shortly by some of our subjects ([ʃət] and [wɒks]), and the vowel in the word *really* was produced as [i] (vowel 1 in Table 9.2). The difficulty some children had with these two vowels can be assigned to the fact that there are no equivalents in P/U.

A final point concerning vowels involves the *addition* of a vowel where none would occur in the speech of a native English speaker (rather than the replacement of one vowel with another). An additional vowel (vowel 12 in Table 9.2) is frequently inserted in the spoken English of all our subjects. Some examples from the data displaying the variety of environments in which it occurs appear below (the vowel is inserted at the point of the hyphen).

Yorkshire children	*Scottish children*
th-ree	g-reen
f-riend	s-weet
b-lue	b-lue
s-phere	-dogs
We(d)n-sday	-sheep

It appears, then, that in the YE data, an extra vowel occurs in a variety of interconsonantal environments irrespective of the nature of the following consonant. This is not the case, though, for the SE data. As in the examples of *green, sweet* and *blue*, the extra vowel was always followed by /r/, /l/ or /w/. This corresponds to the Gaelic rule still influencing SE which requires that if a vowel is to be inserted, then /r/, /l/ or /w/ must follow it. Thus, a native speaker of SE may produce *green, blue* and *sweet* identically to the above. The extra vowel in the Yorkshire data, then, seems to be an influence from P/U, but in the Edinburgh data, it appears to be limited by the constraints of SE phonology.

Dogs and *sheep* are the only examples in our data of an extra vowel appearing in initial position. These were produced by the same speaker, whose mother tongue is Urdu. It is interesting to note that an *initial* extra vowel is a typical feature of the English of speakers whose mother tongue is Hindi-Urdu (e.g. *istation* for 'station'), while speakers whose mother tongue is Panjabi typically insert a vowel *between* two consonants (e.g. *satation* for 'station') (see J.R. Firth, 1948/1973: 62).

Consonants

Although English has more vowels than P/U, it has fewer consonants – RP having 24 consonants, Panjabi 31 and Urdu 36. The 24 consonants of RP are listed in Table 9.3.

Table 9.3 The consonants of RP

	IPA symbol	Example word	Is it in the P/U sound system?
1	p	pea	Yes
2	b	bee	Yes
3	t	tea	Yes
4	d	die	Yes
5	k	key	Yes
6	g	guy	Yes
7	m	me	Yes
8	n	knee	Yes
9	ŋ	sing	Yes
10	f	fee	Yes
11	v	vie	No
12	θ	thigh	No
13	ð	the	No
14	s	see	Yes
15	z	zoo	Yes
16	ʃ	she	Yes
17	ʒ	measure	No
18	h	he	Yes
19	w	we	Near
20	r	rye	Yes
21	j	you	Yes
22	l	lie	Yes
23	tʃ	chew	Yes
24	dʒ	Jew	Yes

The divergence between YE, SE and RP consonants is not nearly so great as that which exists for their vowel systems.

Consonants were affected by the mother tongue sound system more frequently than was the case for vowels. Seven consonants had realisations which constitute transfer from the repertoire of their mother tongue: /p/, /t/, /k/, /θ/, /ð/, /w/, and /r/. These will now be discussed in turn.

In English words beginning with /p/, /t/ or /k/ followed by a vowel, a burst of aspiration follows the /p/, /t/ or /k/ (if spoken by a native speaker). Thus, on placing your hand in front of your lips while saying *pin*, a release of air should be felt after /p/. There appear to be three types of realisation for /p,t,k/ in such positions in our data. That is, the children produce an aspirated consonant, similar to that of a native speaker of English; an unaspirated consonant (making the word *pin* sound closer to *bin*); or a heavily aspirated consonant, the aspiration being greatly in excess of that produced by a native speaker (producing [phɪn]). These productions are due to interference from the mother tongue, as P/U has both aspirated and unaspirated /p,t,k/ in such positions.

All our subjects invariably produce /θ/ as [t], and /ð/ as [d], thereby pronouncing *thumb* as 'tum' and *this* as 'dis'. These realisations constitute transfer from the mother tongue as neither /θ/ nor /ð/ appear in the sound system of P/U.

Similarly, neither /w/ nor /v/ exist in P/U. Instead, there is /ʋ/, which, crudely described, sounds to be halfway between /w/ and /v/. Consequently, the P/U sound was frequently produced by our subjects in words such as *win*, *Wednesday* and *sewing*. (This is sometimes perceived as /v/ by the English ear.)

In P/U, /r/ is usually produced as a weak 'roll' (i.e. the tongue tip taps the roof of the mouth several times in quick succession) or a 'tap' (i.e. the tongue tip taps the roof of the mouth once). When saying English words such as *running*, the children therefore sometimes produced a rolled /r/, and in words such as *green*, a tap was usually produced. Furthermore, if a P/U word contains 'r' in its spelling, that 'r' is always pronounced. This is not always the case in English – for instance, RP and YE speakers do not pronounce the 'r' in words such as *car* (speakers of SE, along with speakers of Irish and American English, on the other hand, do). We found that our subjects frequently pronounced 'r' in English words spelled with one. Examples from the Yorkshire children include *star*, *far*, and *water*. As YE is not an accent which pronounces its 'r's, these productions constitute transfer from the children's mother tongue. Examples from the Scottish children include *car*, *four* and *girl*.

However, as SE *is* 'rhotic' (i.e. 'r'-pronouncing), the speech of our Edinburgh subjects may be containing influence from either P/U *or* SE.

Another effect of the P/U sound system on our subjects' English is the frequent simplification of consonant clusters. Table 9.4 contains examples of all the ways in which consonant clusters were produced when they were realised differently from Standard English.

Table 9.4 Simplification of consonant clusters

Consonant cluster	Target word	Yorks children	Target word	Scot children
$C_1C_2 \rightarrow C_1$	thousand	thousan	thousand	thousan
	Leeds	Leed	Six Grove St.	Sik Grove St.
$C_1C_2C_3 \rightarrow C_2C_3$	crisps	crips		
$C_1C_2C_3 \rightarrow C_2C_1C_2C_3$	crisps	cripsps		
$C_1C_2 \rightarrow C_2C_1$	(medium-)sized	(medium-)sidz	mosque	moks

The majority of these clusters are in final position. Initial clusters were simplified too, but all of them were simplified by the insertion of a vowel between the consonants. These have already been discussed. This accords with Sethi's (1980: 21) claim that insertion of a vowel between consonants is mainly used by Panjabi speakers to simplify *initial* clusters and the elision of one or more consonants is mainly used to simplify *final* consonants.

Final consonant clusters such as /-dz/ and /-ps/ do not occur in native P/U words, which perhaps leads to the omission of final /z/ or /s/ in words such as *Leeds* and *Cleethorpes*. Some of the most difficult final clusters are /-sps/, /-sts/ and /-sks/ (as in *crisps, tests* and *tasks*). Our Yorkshire subjects frequently reduced /-sps/ in crisps to [-ps]. There was one occasion, though, when a very earnest attempt was made to produce /-sps/ - unfortunately, the child tried too hard and produced [-psps]!

Generally, it would appear that the majority of these final consonant cluster simplifications are developmental features – in other words, such features would also frequently be displayed by children who were learning English as their *first* language. However, in specific words (e.g. *mosque*) we posit that the sound system of the mother tongue is the cause of the simplification. It is the following two factors which lead us to this assumption:

- the final cluster of the example word *mosque* is consistently realised as [-ks] by our subjects. On no occasion (by any speaker) is it simplified, for example, to just one consonant, which one might expect if it were a developmental feature;
- the phonological system of P/U does not permit final /-sk/ in its native words. (*Mosque* is not part of the native P/U vocabulary – the P/U word used by our subjects being *masjid*).

Our final observation regarding consonants is that, in all of the data analysed for this paper, there were only two occurrences of a 'retroflex' consonant (in the words *Bradford* and *road*). When a retroflex is produced, the underside of the tongue tip touches the roof of the mouth. The sound system of P/U contains both retroflex /t/ and /d/, and like the non-aspiration of /p,t,k/ discussed above, retroflex consonants are a regular feature of the English spoken by *adults* in Britain whose mother tongue is P/U. There are two questions raised by this:

- Have the children acquired the retroflex consonants in their *mother tongue*?
- Will the P/U spoken in Britain eventually become retroflex-less because of contact with English?

While it would be possible to find a relatively immediate answer to the first question, this is not so for the second. Nevertheless it is reasonable to speculate that this will indeed be the outcome, since the children in our study will clearly have fewer retroflex tokens than their parents or grandparents.

Influence on English spelling

The sound system of the mother tongue does not influence only the *spoken* English of children learning ESOL – it also affects their English *spelling*. The composition below is given to exemplify this. It was written by S.N., an eight-year-old boy at school in Edinburgh. His task was to write about what he had done that weekend. As highlighted in the transcription beneath the passage, his English spelling displays interference from his mother tongue, Panjabi.

'What I did at the weekend' by S.N.

monday 20th. Jauhary.
aim daN in the weceid im go tothe
see saeid ahd im palee ihthe seesaiea
ahd im cam home ahd im eat mi dehare
ahd im waleg tewee ahd im saleepe
ahd i get a dareem ahd im wek ap ih
moneg. wahday im go to bece ahd im sam teg
get to eat im eat a foda hd im palee ih
the bece park ahd im cam hom ahd im
ta eed and im wayre warre saleep
ahd im waek ap ih moneg ahd im direk
tee ahd im eat tost ahd im eat jam.

Key to transcription

a	<a> is written in place of the correct vowel
	Cause: the 'a' vowel in Panjabi has a wide distribution
a̲	a vowel is inserted between two consonants
	Cause: such consonant clusters are not permissible in Panjabi
w̲	<w> is written in place of <v>
	Cause: these are not phonologically distinct in Panjabi

Transcription

aim daN in the weceid im go to the see saeid and im pa̲lee in the see
saied and im cam

I'm done in the weekend I'm go to the seaside and I'm play in the sea-side and I'm come

home and im eat mi denare and im waceg tewee and im sa̲leepe and i
get a da̲reem and

home and I'm eat my dinner and I'm watching TV and I'm sleep(y) and I get a dream and

im wek ap in moneg. wan day im go to bece and im sam teg get to eat im eat a

I'm wake up in morning. One day I'm go to beach and I'm something get to eat I'm eat a

fod and im p<u>a</u>lee in the bece park and im cam hom and im taeed and im <u>w</u>arre <u>w</u>arre

food and I'm play in the beach park and I'm come home and I'm tired and I'm very very

s<u>a</u>leep and im waek ap in moneg and im d<u>i</u>rek tee and im eat tost and im eat Jam.

sleep and I'm wake up in morning and I'm drink tea and I'm eat toast and I'm eat jam.

The influence of Yorkshire/Scottish English

Having exemplified ways in which the mother tongue of our subjects affected their English, we will now consider the extent of the influence of the local variety of English to which they are exposed.

Vowels

We found that 15 of the 20 English vowels were frequently realised in a manner identical to the way in which they would be produced in the regional accent of their monolingual English-speaking peers. For instance, our subjects in West Yorkshire pronounced the following words with YE vowels: *party* [pronounced with vowel 2 in Table 9.2 above]; *class* [vowel 4]; *buttons* [vowel 8]; *page* [monophthong]; and *yellow* [vowel 12]. And our subjects in Edinburgh pronounced the following words with SE vowels: *sleep* [short]; *him* [centralised]; *can't* [vowel 4]; *dogs* [vowel 7]; *four* [vowel 20]; *zoo* [high, fronted]; and *person* [lengthened vowel 3].

Consonants

We found that 7 of the 24 English consonants were influenced by the local variety of English. For instance, our subjects in West Yorkshire pronounced the following words with YE consonants: *water* [glottal stop]; *Bradford* [held, unreleased closure, sounding similar to a glottal stop – see S.A. Firth, 1991: 24]; and *recording* [n]. And our subjects in Edinburgh pronounced the following words with SE consonants: *fit* [glottal stop]; *first* [retracted – Sean Connery style]; *scarves* [f]; and *ears* [s, instead of z].

It is perhaps of no great surprise that more vowels are influenced by the local English variety than consonants, as this reflects the fact that 'The chief source of segmental variation among accents is in vowel quality' (Hawkins, 1984: 232).

Conclusion

We have shown that gross generalisations should not be made about the phonological development of ESOL learners living in Britain. Both the impact of the local variety of English, especially the impact of vowels, and the influence of their particular mother tongue have a great effect. The general trend in the English speech of our 17 subjects seems to be that:

- When they *do* adapt, they adapt to the features of the particular *local* variety of English to which they are exposed (Yorkshire English or Scottish English). That is, *in terms of acts of identity, they assimilate to their monolingual English-speaking peer group.*
- When they do *not* adapt, they transfer features from the sound system of their mother tongue (Panjabi/Urdu). That is, *they preserve their ethnic identity through the accent of English spoken by South Asian adults.*

The implications of these findings *vis à vis* the National Curriculum are worrying. The 1993 National Curriculum document, *English for ages 5 to 16*, recommends proficiency in Standard English by the end of Key Stage 2 (i.e. by the age of 11). As a result, children whose English contains features both from the local accent and from their mother tongue will be at a disadvantage when assessed, as they are in danger of being marked down because of this.

We are currently in the midst of a whole movement towards monolingual, monodialectal schooling for the children of England. This is reinforced by the fact that the 1993 document, unlike the previous 1989 version, makes no mention of bilingual children at all. This issue is discussed further in Verma, Corrigan and Firth (in press). Due to these educational changes, it seems that the inevitable conclusion is one which has been noted by Edwards and Alladina (1991: 24–25), namely that:

> We may well be on target for a return to the pathological model of language [English] where any speaker – working class, Black, or bilingual – who departs from the norm is labelled as deficient.

Note

This paper is based on material in the paper 'The developing phonological system of Panjabi/Urdu speaking children learning English as a second language in Britain' by Mahendra K. Verma, Karen P. Corrigan and Sally Firth in Leather, J. & James, A. (eds) (1992) *New Sounds 92: Proceedings of the 1992 Amsterdam Symposium on the Acquisition of Second Language Speech*. Amsterdam: University of Amsterdam.

References

Agnihotri, R.K. (1979) Processes of assimilation: A sociolinguistic study of Sikh children in Leeds. PhD thesis, University of York.

Bansal, R.K. (1969) *The Intelligibility of Indian English.* Hyderabad: Central Institute of English.

—(1983) *Studies in Phonetics and Spoken English.* Hyderabad: Central Institute of English and Foreign Languages.

Barron, A.W.J. (1961a) English vowels for Indian learners. *Bulletin of the Central Institute of English* 1, 77–83.

—(1961b) The English dental fricatives in India. *Bulletin of the Central Institute of English* 1, 84–6.

Department for Education and the Welsh Office (1993) *English for ages 5 to 16.* London: HMSO.

Edwards, V. and Alladina, S. (1991) Many people, many tongues: Babel and beyond. In Alladina, S. and V. Edwards (eds) *Multilingualism in the British Isles* 2: Africa, the Middle East and Asia. London and New York: Longman.

Firth, J.R. (1948) Sounds and prosodies. In W.E. Jones and J. Laver (eds) (1973) *Phonetics in Linguistics. A Book of Readings.* London and New York: Longman. Also in Palmer, F.R. (ed.) (1970) *Prosodic Analysis.* London: Oxford University Press.

Firth, S.A. (1991) *Yorkshire Assimilation.* Unpublished manuscript, University of York.

Gimson, A.C. (1980) *An Introduction to the Pronunciation of English.* (3rd edn) London: Edward Arnold.

Hawkins, P. (1984) *Introducing Phonology.* London: Hutchinson.

Pandit, P.B. (1964) Indian readjustments in the English consonant system. *Indian Linguistics* 25, 202–5.

Rao, K.S.N. (1961) A footnote to the Indian pronunciation of the initial /k t p/ and /v/ and /w/ in English. *Indian Linguistics* 22, 160–3.

Sethi, J. (1978) The vowel system in educated Panjabi-speakers' English. *CIEFL Bulletin* 14 (2), 35–48.

—(1979) The consonant system in educated Panjabi-speakers' English. *CIEFL Bulletin* 15 (2), 21–36.

—(1980) Consonant clusters in educated Panjabi-speakers' English. *CIEFL Bulletin* 16 (1), 7–29.

Tough, J. (1985) *Talk Two: Children using English as a Second Language in Primary Schools.* London: Onyx Press.

Varma, S. (1957) The pronunciation of English in North-Western India. *Indian Linguistics* 18, 86–8.

Verma, M.K., Corrigan, K.P. and Firth, S.A. (in press) Death by education: The plight of community languages in Britain. *Language Issues.*

Wells, J.C. (1982a) *Accents of English 2: The British Isles.* Cambridge: Cambridge University Press.

—(1982b) *Accents of English 3: Beyond the British Isles.* Cambridge: Cambridge University Press.

10 Bilingual Children and their Assessment through Mother Tongue

JEAN MILLS

This paper takes the question of fairness as its theme. It asks how primary school teachers can help developing bilingual children to perform to the best of their ability during assessment. Several factors are put forward to be taken into consideration: (a) the range of children's linguistic repertoire; (b) differential performance due to mood, context and audience; (c) the use of fair settings. These points are illuminated by the description of a small-scale project involving SAT assessment at Key Stage One. This brings into focus unavoidable problems of cultural bias, and seeks to establish situations where mother tongue assessment might be most appropriate.

Assessment Issues

How do we, as primary school teachers, assess oral language? Do we use tick-off categories on checklists? Do we analyse transcripts of tape recordings? Do we monitor with ongoing judgements as the spoken language is uttered? Perhaps we use combinations of all these, but experience over the past 20 years indicates just how difficult the task is.

Even the Assessment of Performance Unit (APU) surveys during the 1980s, using a fairly structured technique, only attempted to assess 11 year olds in the primary range – and even then within a circumscribed set of categories (viz. Instructing/Directing, Giving and Interpreting Information, Narrating, Describing, Discussing). How much more difficult it is to achieve anything comprehensive across the age and ability range, when children in the same class speak two or three different languages.

Where, then, can bilingual assessment begin, and what do we mean when we use that term? Does it refer to:

(i) the assessment of specific abilities (such as maths or history concepts) through the mother tongue; or
(ii) the more general assessment of a child's linguistic abilities in English and in their mother tongue?

Whichever it is, we are looking for a fair assessment of children's abilities and, therefore, assessment of standard English is only one dimension of a child's all-round language abilities. Some children have a very wide linguistic repertoire, made up of several language varieties. The very term 'bilingual' (Baetens Beardsmore, 1986: Chapter 1) may obscure this since it is often used in a loose and imprecise way to refer to dual-language users in inner-city schools. We are not talking about a homogeneous group.

In fact, such children may have high level oracy and literacy skills in two or more languages; or a basic command of one language with more developed skills in another; or oral fluency in two languages but selective use of each according to setting (e.g. playground/classroom/home) or function (e.g. personal/academic). Thus, Bourne's definition: 'Bilingualism stands for the alternate use of two languages in the same individual' (1988: 1–2), is followed by a caveat about assuming that the term indicates equal proficiency or that it offers any judgement about the range or quality of a child's linguistic skills.

Some children have abilities which are only apparent in one language. Many of us have had experience of meeting children who are monosyllabic in English but can carry out lengthy and involved conversations in another tongue, or children who are very able in English but who cannot communicate well in their first language. Similarly, some children have abilities which transfer across language boundaries; they can describe, report incidents, and tell stories in two languages.

Here, for example, six year old Shahira is composing a story *extempore*. She started in English and continued in Pushtu:

> He knocked on Number One's door. He said 'May I have a glass of water?' They opened it a little, 'Come in'. They thought it was a man, a nice kind man... (*then in Pushtu*)... He didn't really want some water. He came in and got the knife and killed her.'

On the other hand, I encountered Kuldip (aged six) who was a Panjabi-speaker and had been in the UK for six months. It became evident Kuldip did not know the names of the shapes 'square' and 'rectangle' in Panjabi, but *did* know them in English. This illustrates the phenomenon identified by Appel & Muysken (1987: 165) of lexical transfer from the second into the first language in the form of loan words. But, more than this, it reveals how inappropriate it is to test all non-English speakers in Panjabi, when particular children may be able to name certain attributes in one language only. Such an example of 'interlanguage strategy' (Appel & Muysken,1987: 83) highlights the need for National Curriculum guidelines to clarify the circumstances in which children should be assessed through their mother tongue. These will vary from person to person and situation to situation.

There are obvious implications for the administration of SATs (Standard Assessment Tasks). My experience of implementing SATs using bilingual communicators suggests that not all developing bilingual children benefit, either from having those assessment tasks conducted in English, or having them translated into their mother tongue. In each case, the language used needs to be matched appropriately to the child. Such matching depends on the pre-existence of an adequate language profile for individual children, as discussed below.

Furthermore, all children reveal differences in performance according to their mood, their relationship with other speakers, or the setting in which they perform. This variability is recognised in the National Curriculum which asks for a range of situations, audiences, and activities (1995:2).

For example, Ranjit (aged five) would often refuse to communicate in a one-to-one teaching situation. On her own, talking to herself while sorting set rings, she says:

> Circle, circle... Each Peach Pear Plum... I know what you're writing (*balances a ring on her head*)... look, don't fall down... I'm gonna have the orange... (*makes a pattern of rings*)... two eyes, one nose, a snowman... it's nearly snowing.

Similarly, Nazma (aged seven), who was always mute in the presence of a teacher in school, and who would read her book in English in a whisper to a friend, was observed chatting and playing happily at break-time, and at home spoke in Bengali to her family in front of the home-school liaison teacher. All these details could figure in any language profile of Nazma. The presence of another language, in her case Bengali, adds a further dimension to what has been labelled 'differential performance' (Clark, 1988: 43).

Obviously, children are sensitive to the settings in which they use English and in which they use their mother tongue. Many children are quite relaxed in using their first language in the playground or for social interchange in the classroom. What may be more difficult is for them to use that language formally or academically, such as greeting parents in assembly and participating in class lessons.

The policy of the school needs to be quite clear on this matter, so that children come to know when it is appropriate for them to use their mother tongue. Such occasions could be during:

- news time;
- singing songs and rhymes;
- story-telling by older to younger children;
- interviews;
- role play;
- translation of books;
- small group discussion of tasks.

This may take some time to achieve. For example, a bilingual colleague has expressed disappointment to me that, during her first term in a new school, children would not use their mother tongue at all. Another colleague discovered that children replied in English until she continually reminded them that they could reply in Panjabi. Only after three years in her present post does she find that children now habitually speak to her in their mother tongue. Thus, for some children, a favourable context must include the relationship they have developed with a familiar adult. It is not enough to exhort them to speak Panjabi in school and expect an immediate response.

If children do not use their mother tongue when they are encouraged to do so, teachers will speculate on the reasons. Is it because the school has somehow conveyed negative messages? Is it because the mother tongue has come to be regarded as the language of home and English as the language of school? Is it because parents have given particular instructions?

Whatever the reasons, the effect will be that teachers will have a limited view of the abilities of particular children. The effect on the children will be that they miss out on opportunities to practise certain skills through their mother tongue. This, in turn, may affect their development in English. After all, if a child has no chance to explain a sequence of events in a science activity, perhaps to another child who could translate, the development of this particular language skill may well be delayed.

Certain settings also particularly to encourage use of the mother tongue. Observation of Reception and Year One children over several weeks identified the following situations as being especially conducive:

- domestic role play;
- imaginative play with models and construction toys;
- pair work, especially when planning or playing a game;
- working with a bilingual student or other adult;
- cooking a familiar dish.

All these seemed to be 'fair' settings in two ways. They were 'fair' in that the use of the mother tongue in such situations was appropriate, relaxed and natural; the children were not under pressure. They were also 'fair' in that the children were using language in situations where they were entirely competent and at ease. They could appear at their best.

SATs and Mother Tongue Assessment

How far, then, are children helped when SAT assessment is carried out in their mother tongue? In 1992, I was in charge of a small-scale project involving seven bilingual classroom assistants and 14 ESL teachers in six schools. The description which follows brings together several of the issues involved in mother tongue assessment.

Evidence collected

School A, SAT SC9, Language: Panjabi, three Year 1 children aged six

The children had worked with the bilingual assistant the previous year and were happy and relaxed with her. The assessment took place in the school library.

At a preliminary session, the teachers played a domino game which used different sets of outdoor clothes (relevant because the SAT was about different types of weather). The game ensured that the children were soon chattering away spontaneously in English. Although the teachers and assistant had prepared a script in English and Panjabi, they found they had to deviate from it at times, especially when the children had difficulty in talking about changes in the weather and the effects it had on their lives.

Throughout, the children seemed happier replying in English, even when spoken to in Panjabi. Occasionally, they offered Panjabi words when they did not know the English (such as 'mi' for 'rain') or used a key English word in a Panjabi sentence: 'when it's cold'. One child confused the English words 'hot' and 'cold', but knew the difference in Panjabi. The consensus in this group was that Panjabi acted in a supportive role and its use depended on the children's familiarity with using it in school.

School B, SAT SC6, Language: Panjabi and Urdu, five Year 2 children aged seven

In the week prior to the assessment, the children were introduced to the room where they would work. Objects which were mostly familiar to them were chosen, although two (a cone and a cork) which the children might not have encountered were included, to assess to what extent they had grasped a particular concept. Otherwise, the objects did not appear to present any cultural problems, nor did the assistant have difficulty naming them in the mother tongue. The activities were introduced to the children as a game, and they were told they were going to speak English and Panjabi. Although the group had a script, it was used more as an outline. Occasionally, English phrases with Panjabi translations were added to make the instructions clearer.

Most children chose to answer in English, although all used both languages at times. Naming the objects was difficult because not all the children had the necessary vocabulary in their mother tongue. Several were confused by the cone and the cork. One child, in particular, was initially reluctant to speak but appeared encouraged to participate by the use of Panjabi. He was able to name all the objects in both English and Panjabi. The opinion of the staff was that the two languages reinforced each other:

> We saw a marked increase in confidence by the children..... the activity was grasped quickly because they could understand what was expected of them. We felt the use of both languages gave a greater chance of success to the children. S and A would not have responded or participated fully if there had not been a bilingual input.

School C, SAT SC6, Language: Mirpuri Panjabi, three Year 3 children aged eight, including two newly arrived (one, one month earlier, and the other, just under a year ago)

The SC6 task had been chosen because the researchers felt that:

- the children could handle materials which were known to them;
- the task was less culturally biased than SC9;
- success depended less on memory than for SC9;
- there were problems in translating weather terms.

The Year 3 children were chosen because they were known by two of the researchers. The staff did not want to cause disruption to Year 2, who were already involved with SATs. All the children lacked fluency in English.

This group split into three. Each researcher assessed one child individually in English using a script. The children then returned to the classroom assistant, who repeated the test in Panjabi.

At Level 1, child A could not describe any objects in English but understood enough to try desperately to signal what he meant. Child B could only use the English word 'heavy'. Both boys easily completed the assessment using Panjabi. Child C improved her descriptions using Panjabi. At Level 2, child C corrected an error on her worksheet after hearing the Panjabi instruction. Child A could not explain his sorting in English, but, using Panjabi, clarified his thoughts and thus moved an object placed inappropriately (i.e. 'can/cannot be broken'). Child B sorted his groups to 'smooth' and 'rough'. Child C also re-classified her objects in Panjabi and labelled them 'made by people' and 'found in the garden'. Although the children did not complete the Level 3 part of the SAT, they were able to give more differences and similarities in Panjabi than in English. They were thus assessed as 'working towards' this level.

The evidence of these researchers showed the clearest indications of the benefits of bilingually assessing children with limited English. This was not clear in the other schools, where the children had generally been born in England and all understood and spoke English fairly well, but it was noted that, because the children could clarify their thoughts using their mother tongue, they were able to correct their misunderstandings. The report concluded:

We believe that all children should be tested in their preferred tongue.

This, of course, might be either English or Panjabi, whichever the child felt more confident in using at school.

Discussion

Since this investigation involved only some 22 adults and 20 children, the small scale renders any conclusions tentative. However, several points did recur and I feel justified in emphasising them – especially as the area of mother tongue assessment is relatively unexplored. Overall, there were favourable and unfavourable aspects to the assessments carried out by the teachers.

Unfavourable aspects

(1) Generally, the teachers discovered, as I had in my own work, that there were problems with certain features of these SATs even before the bilingual issue was considered – for example, in the case of SC6 Materials, Level 2.

The teacher was asked to help the child sort a collection of 10 objects into groups according to what they were made of (e.g. wood, metal, etc.). The children were then asked to sort the collection according to any characteristic of the materials (e.g. texture, weight, hardness, etc.). In my experience, children were confused by the preliminary sorting; by uncertainty as to why further classification was needed; and by being required to sort the objects again, this time according to type or colour rather than property.

Similarly, in SC9 Level 1 and Level 2, children were asked to recall types of weather (i.e. yesterday, last week, on a school trip, or on their birthday). This put the emphasis on memory rather than on the concept. After all, which of us can remember what the weather was like on our birthday, or on Christmas day? It was also difficult for children to differentiate between the weather in spring and autumn.

(2) The SATs were not straightforward in cultural or linguistic terms. This was particularly true for SC9: Earth and Atmosphere. The following difficulties were encountered:

- Some teachers were unfamiliar with the items and the Panjabi names for the children's clothes, so that it was difficult at times to use contrasting clothing to explain the difference between summer and winter clothes. In any case, many children wore similar clothes all year round.
- There were no equivalent words in Panjabi and Urdu for the names of the four seasons, nor for snow, thunderstorm or sleet; a phrase or further explanation had to be used. This could obviously lead to a lack of precision in assessing concepts in this area.
- There was doubt about how helpful it was to children born in England to be assessed through a mother tongue which expresses weather concepts quite differently.
- For SC6 to avoid confusion or incomprehension, the objects needed to be chosen carefully.

Favourable aspects

(1) Languages must be correctly matched. This may seem obvious but the Panjabi-speaking teacher in the group stressed that it is confusing and inappropriate, for example, for Mirpuri-speaking children to be assessed in Urdu, or Sikh Panjabi-speakers to encounter Mirpuri Panjabi.

(2) A supportive context. All groups took care to make the situation as comfortable as possible for the children. For instance, there was always at least one adult present whom they knew. Each group of researchers set up preliminary sessions in which they played or talked with the children in the room which was to be used for the test. The activity itself was often presented in the form of a game. Familiar objects from the classroom were usually chosen.

(3) Familiarity with the bilingual assistant. This worked in several ways. Some assistants who knew the teachers and children adapted their interventions according to when they judged that further explanations would be most supportive to the child. Some assistants had additional insights into the children's abilities because they had often worked with them in their mother tongue in Reception classes. Others had translated for parents, or lived in the local community themselves. Assistants were able to relate the tasks to the children's experiences. For example, when one child was asked to put a tick by an object which would burn away if it was made very hot, the assistant added 'like a shalwar on a fire'.

(4) Role of the mother tongue. Obviously, mother tongue assessment is helpful where a child's English is not sufficiently developed to understand the task. This was amply demonstrated in School C. However, a more subtle and intriguing role was indicated in other schools. This was the supportive and confirming role of the children's first language, especially when they were not confident or inexperienced. So although many children preferred to answer in English despite the presence of a communicator, several were visibly more assured in responding when their mother tongue was used to confirm the question or instruction they received. This finding is in line with evidence (cited by Cook, 1991 viz. Dornic, 1969; Magiste, 1979; and Marsh and Maki, 1978), that learners are less confident in grappling with cognitive processes using their second language until they have been learning it for four to six years.

Furthermore, for many of the children, English was clearly their preferred language for school. They were either not at ease using Panjabi or did not realise they could use it in school. One child, for example, had to be reminded to use the Urdu word for 'bangle' when she did not know the English. In contrast, however, several did not know the English equivalent. They were flexible in using their languages. It was important for these children that they exercised this option, since it gave them a greater chance of success. It would obviously help them to be told that they have the choice of using either or both of their languages during assessment. (Given present constraints on staffing, few schools can achieve this ideal situation.)

Finally, the children in school were able to correct their errors when they had the opportunity to reason in their mother tongue. This was despite the fact that they would not have been taught the SAT tasks in their mother tongue. This brings into question the blanket assumption that it is unfair to test children in their mother tongue unless they have been taught in it. I would suggest that doing tasks which depend on reasoning, logical thought, or 'talking through', the stronger language greatly helps the child. Certain SATs, especially in Maths and Science, particularly lend themselves to this and we need to identify which those are.

Implications for Schools

(1) Information about individual children's use of their languages differed. Some clearly preferred English; some moved flexibly between languages; some performed better with their mother tongue as support. To gain some indication of where children are on this spectrum, schools need to collect information from Nursery/ Reception onwards about children's language use, and include this in their formative assessments. Some schools in the survey did this on a regular basis.

(2) Monolingual teachers need in-service training about how to make use of bilingual assistance. There was evidence that, in some schools, a lack of flexibility in time-tabling and/or deployment of bilingual classroom assistants inhibited their playing a full role in assessing children's abilities.

(3) The role of bilingual assistants was crucial and, clearly, several had considerable expertise in this area. Sometimes they had insights about certain children because they had worked in their mother tongue with them from an early age; they had translated for sensitive family matters; or they belonged to the local community. This supportive role has implications for the training of bilingual assistants.

- How far are they going to be involved in assessment?
- What forms of involvement will be appropriate?
- What opportunities will there be to discuss translation options and implications, both before and after an assessment?

How best may bilingual assistants be sensitised to the subtleties of the engagement?

However, which agency is ready and willing to take on this training role, given LEA fragmentation, lack of resources, the pressure of other priorities and the differentiation between the roles of teachers and assistants? Much more needs to be done if developing bilinguals are to be given a fair deal in formal assessment.

Acknowledgements

This paper is based on material which appeared in R.W. Mills and J. Mills (1993) *Bilingualism in the Primary School* (London: Routledge) and *Multicultural Teaching* 11 (2) (1993), re-printed by kind permission of the editor, Gillian Klein.

References

Appel, R. and Muysken, P. (1987) *Language Contact and Bilingualism*. London: Edward Arnold.
A.P.U. (1986) *Speaking and Listening: Assessment at Age 11*.Windsor: NFER-Nelson.
Baetens Beardsmore, H. (1986) *Bilingualism: Basic Principles*. Clevedon: Multilingual Matters.
Bourne, J. (1989) *Moving into the Mainstream: LEA Provision for Bilingual Pupils*. Windsor: NFER-Nelson.
Clark, M. (1988) *Children under Five: Educational Research and Evidence*. London: Gordon & Breach.
Cook, V. (1991) *Second Language Learning and Teaching*. London: Edward Arnold.
Great Britain. Department for Education (1995) *Key Stages 1 and 2 of the National Curriculum*. London: HMSO.

11 Oracy Issues in ESL Teaching in Key Stage 2: Using the Language Master as a Bridge Between Non-standard and Standard English

MARY ROSE PEATE

Oracy has become the accepted term in educational theory for the fluent, confident and correct use of the standard spoken form of English; it appears alongside literacy and numeracy as one of the three essential skills to be acquired as a result of schooling. To a large extent, however, the particular strategies required to teach both oracy and literacy to speakers of English as a second language have been ignored. This paper will describe materials developed as a result of my secondment to the National Oracy Project which I have used to teach and to assess English as a second language in the primary school.

I will begin by defining some of the terms used in the title of this paper, such as 'oracy', 'the Language Master' and, above all, 'Standard English', in the context of teaching English as a Second Language (ESL) to bilingual children. Indeed, the reader may well have doubts about whether those working with bilingual children should be concentrating primarily on insisting that they use 'Standard English' as the only truly acceptable form of classroom communication. The making of errors is a necessary part of language learning, according to Dulay & Burt (1974), since 'you can't learn without goofing'. However, the latest Orders for English in the National Curriculum from the Department for Education seem to indicate that, at least for the time being, that particular debate is suspended.

> Ours not to reason why;
> Ours but to do or die,

as the soldiers of the Light Brigade reflected, before advancing into the path of the enemy guns!

Trudgill (1975) trounces Wilkinson (1963) who first introduced the concept of 'oracy' into educational theory. What Wilkinson seems to mean by 'oracy' is the fluent, confident and correct use of the standard spoken form of one's native language. He sets it alongside literacy and numeracy as one of the three essential skills to be acquired by children as a result of their schooling. His concern is with the English language only, and with native speakers of English at that. In fact, he specifically excludes second-language learners and children with Special Educational Needs, particularly deafness, from the scope of his argument that a command of the standard form of the language can be *taught*. He refers to the type of educated speaker that he is himself as 'Linguistic Man' and to the speaker of a non-standard variety as 'Non-linguistic Man', the doer rather than the sayer. He considers himself to be relating the early Bernstein theories of the Elaborated and Restricted codes to actual pedagogic practice.

Describing Wilkinson as 'a notable offender' in encouraging crude 'misperceptions' of Bernstein's theory among teachers, Trudgill states: 'Wilkinson gives the impression that there is some necessary connection between "code" and "dialect", which there is not.' (1975: 92). He also deplores Wilkinson's free use of the terms 'linguistically deprived' and 'linguistically disadvantaged' to describe non-standard usage.

The term 'oracy', despite all these reservations, 'caught on' with teachers, and other sociolinguists such as Stubbs, Crystal and Lesley Milroy have attempted to develop and refine the concept. Trudgill's warnings do need to be heeded, however, as Ashworth (1988) points out. Inspired by the work of Vygotsky and of Bruner, 'who sees language as extending and amplifying both cognition and cognitive development' (1988: 139), Ashworth states that Tough, in her work for the Schools Council on oracy (1977), developed:

> dialogue strategies, which are to be used by the teacher, [which] are open to serious objection [in] that they are likely to result in catechetical interviews between the teacher and the child, with the teacher in the role of initiator and the child in that of responder... the child is given little guidance on how to conduct a conversation, how to start it, how to finish it or how to sustain it. (1988: 47)

The National Oracy Project was set up in 1987, by the School Curriculum Development Committee. The Kent Oracy Project followed

in 1988, funded by the National Curriculum Council. I was recruited to
the Kent Oracy Project in its opening (research) phase, as one of a team of
three who were concerned with ways of promoting the development of
oracy in children with Special Educational Needs and those for whom
English is a Second Language. The other two were a Section 11 teacher
recently moved to North Kent from Bradford and the deputy head of a
small Special School. I was at that time an ESL support tutor in a rather
unusual village school where one pupil in six (32 children from a roll of
180) came from countries other than England. About 12 different first
languages were spoken: European, African, Asian and South American.
The children were not born in England; they were only with us for
periods of time varying from one to five years, accompanying their
parents who were postgraduate students at the University College
situated in the village. These parents had high academic expectations
and were very supportive, especially of the learning of English as an
addition to their children's language repertoires. Many of the older
children were already literate in other languages, but faced the problems
posed by interrupted schooling of any kind, particularly the difficulties of
maintaining progress in different school settings and of re-integration on
their return to the home country.

I was concerned that the advice being given to teachers in, for
example, *Teaching Talking and Learning* by the National Oracy Project,
was that:

> Welsh/English bilingualism is officially recognised in the National
> Curriculum for Wales, with special arrangements being made for the
> assessment of Welsh-speaking children in English-medium schools,
> [but] other bilingual children, even if they start school with very little
> English, are expected to reach the same attainment levels as
> monolingual English speakers. Their stage of development in English
> may affect not only their rating in that language but in other subjects
> as well. (1990: 24)

Although strategies are suggested in the same document for improving oral fluency in native speakers who have been observed not to be
communicating as well as their peers, no suggestions at all are made for
teaching English to children who do not speak the language. Respect for
the first language is stressed, as is the importance of 'encouraging
children to use their preferred language for talking through ideas'
(1990: 25), where several children speak the same language, or 'where
adult support is available in the home language' (1990: 26), but no
mention is made of strategies for *teaching* the second language. Bilingual

parents are seen as the main resource available to the class teacher, given that each bilingual child is likely to have at least one parent who speaks 'the home language', where that is not English.

In the case of English children learning Welsh and French *in school*, resources (i.e. methods and materials) are regarded as vital to effective teaching. There were no materials for teaching the children with whom I was working. I used *Scope*, but it was seriously out of date. The Language Master Course, *Let's Speak English*, was of the same vintage (early 1960s), and has indeed now been withdrawn by the publishers, Drake Educational Associates. They no longer provide a course of this type, offering the opinion that ESL teachers prefer to make their own materials. That did not seem to me to be the case, but that was apparently what I would have to do.

I would be in good company. Bilingual support teachers were praised by Silvaine Wiles HMI during the 1992 'Working with Bilingual Children' INSET in York for their ingenuity in devising materials for teaching English, since none are commercially available. She pointed out that the materials were so good that everybody used them. This seemed to imply that the materials were of use in teaching language skills to monolingual children too. It is surprising to speakers of other languages that the English do not seem to *teach* their language to native speakers. The policy-makers have set up frameworks, including the latest Orders, which effectively reward the fluent standard speaker and penalise all others.

In *Teaching Talking and Learning* (1990), the NCC publication from the second (dissemination) phase of the Project, quoted above, good practice was reported in setting up real 'speaking and listening' tasks with real outcomes, where:

> Talk is often the vehicle for achieving another purpose. Teachers in the Oracy Project have found lots of useful purposes for children's talk by handing over to children some of their own uses of talk, e.g. taking messages to other teachers, answering the telephone, showing round visitors, explaining work to parents. (1990: 31)

It seemed to me that it would be very difficult for beginner bilinguals to carry out the activities suggested, while they were still struggling to understand and be understood. I decided to try to observe how often non-native speakers were permitted by their peers and by their teachers to be active rather than passive speech-partners. Did they manage to question, to interrupt, to argue and persuade, to introduce new topics and generally take the initiative when using their second language with native speakers? Most importantly, were they encouraged and enabled to make clear when they did not understand, to seek repair in faulty communication? Were they being *taught* the new language, as were English monolingual beginners in French or Welsh? Were they experiencing 'immersion education' or was it more like submersion, sinking without a lifebelt?

Large group or whole class settings seemed to be the most problematic, particularly if the non-native speaker was asked to contribute *first*, before any of the other children had spoken, so that no model of structure had been set in place. Milroy comments:

> If we are to obtain any kind of insight into the structure of everyday spoken language, we need to look at speech where the speaker has selected his own topic which does not emerge as a result of direct questioning. (1987: 59)

It seems to me to follow that the situation of talking in small groups of equals is more likely to encourage natural language acquisition than taking part in the unequal dyad of active adult and passive child which is customary in the classroom, even outside Ashworth's 'catechetical interviews'. Milroy points out that a true group can be as small as three persons, providing that this is permitted to have the effect of 'outnumbering the interviewer and decreasing the likelihood that speakers will simply wait for questions to which they articulate responses.' (1987: 62)

I have used the term 'equal' rather than 'peer', because all children need to experience 'opportunities to hear their teacher [and other adults] talk politely but also informally when appropriate' (National Oracy Project, 1990: 21).

As well as eavesdropping on conversation of the kind described, children also need to take part in it, but not all young children are naturally courteous. Most need the experience of having their teacher 'model the courtesy and ability to listen that [she] expects them to adopt with each other' (National Oracy Project, 1990: 21). This may run counter to the urge to intervene, 'to encourage careful, standardized styles and inhibit the emergence of vernacular structures' (Milroy, 1987: 211), but can be demonstrated to be more productive. Unfortunately, the recent pronouncements on the need to insist on the use of Standard English even in the playground obviously seek to pre-empt the discussion. This insistence has serious limitations as an approach to facilitating 'language for thinking' and 'language for doing' in the primary school, 'particularly in the case of bilingual children whose "receptive" English (what they can understand) will almost always be ahead of their "productive" language (what they can say).' (National Oracy Project, 1990: 41)

Milroy (1987: 199–212) analyses the effectiveness of some language assessment procedures currently in use in American schools and their possible relevance to Britain. These procedures are triple-pronged, involving:

(1) A group interview where an adult attempts to encourage conversation among members of the child peer-group.
(2) A peer conference where children are left alone with a school-like task for about 10 minutes (they are asked to construct a story to match comic-strip pictures);
(3) A test interview, where a standardised test is administered to an individual child. (See Milroy, 1987: 208)

As far as modifying traditional classroom practice is concerned, she highlights two particular mismatches between teachers' expectation of children and their established patterns of communication, which repeatedly cause problems with multilingual and 'low-status' indigenous schoolchildren:

(1) Failure to understand the adult's apparent request for information as an actual invitation to perform, to display implicit knowledge orally: pseudo-questions.
(2) Reluctance to give an audible running commentary on problem-solving activities, when they may have been trained to be seen and not heard in the presence of adults.

Inspired by these suggestions, I devised a pilot oral assessment exercise, or 'standardised test', and tried it out with the 32 children of the postgraduates from overseas, who ranged in age from five to 11. I attempted, as naturally as possible, to use the same 'script' with each child, so that comparison was possible when playing back the tapes. Any variation was therefore being initiated by the child. The opening section follows:

An oral assessment exercise – one-to-one

An attractive commercial book-and-tape pack is presented upside-down on a table or desk, with the instruction written on the cardboard backing:
Please look inside the bag.

There is a carrier bag underneath the pack, on the desktop.

Teacher:	Can you see any writing?
	Can you tell me what it says?
(If necessary):	Shall I read it to you?
	Is there a bag there?
	Where is it?
(If child only points):	Yes, it's underneath.
	There's the bag.
	Is it a funny-looking bag?
(If necessary):	What's funny about it?

The carrier bag is one advertising W.H.Smith's, and has a face on it consisting of a nose made from a pencil-sharpener, eyes of pencil-shavings and a mouth of a pencil-case, containing two pencils. The teacher encourages the child to describe this and discuss it as fully as age, maturity and competence allow, but with the minimum of prompting. This action functions as a deliberate distraction and delaying tactic before the child is called upon to carry out the initial instruction.

Teacher:	Can you remember what the writing told you to do?
(Recall if necessary)	If there is anything in there, you can take it out.
(The bag contains a folded sheet of paper.)	
	Is it the right way up?
(Ensuring paper is upside-down)	
	What do we call that, when something's the wrong way up?
	Can you see any more writing? What does it say?
(If necessary):	Shall I read it for you?
(Child may join in)	The writing says: Can you get baby black rabbit to his food? Do you know what rabbits eat?
(Prompt, if necessary)	
	Can you see any rabbit food in the picture?
(If necessary):	Shall I show you?
Teacher:	Yes, it's a long way from the baby rabbit. Where do rabbits live?
(Prompt, if necessary)	
(Pointing under desk)	
	If you were a rabbit in a tunnel and you met some fallen stones or a creature, could you jump over it? Why not? If you tried to jump over it what would happen?

WAIT WHILE CHILD THINKS

So if the baby black rabbit meets a spider he can't jump over it...
or if he meets a snake he can't jump over it or if he meets some rocks and stones fallen down...

(Pause, hoping child will join in)

he can't jump over it
or if he comes to where the tree roots have grown down and blocked the way, here and here and here...

(Pause, hoping child will take over)

he can't jump over it.
He'll have to go back and try another way.

(If still solo):

And if he meets a frog, or a snail he can't jump over it and if he meets a weasel...

(Pause, allowing child to elaborate)

(If necessary):

he can't jump over it or the weasel might bite him and fight him. So will you make your finger into the baby black rabbit, and go along the white path, and show me how he gets to his food?

WAIT WHILE THE CHILD THINKS

Encourage progress once the child starts, but try to resist giving further clues. Some children see at once that the rabbit will have to go up out of the tunnel, cross some grass, and go down another hole. If they do, the teacher should praise them and then ask:

How did you do that?
What's that at the top, then?
Can rabbits go up from underground, then, and run over the grass?

All children should be praised for their efforts and if necessary cautioned to secrecy until 'everybody's done it'. Ideally, if used with a group of children for purposes of comparison, one child's attempt should follow directly on another's. There is more, but that much probably gives the general idea.

My script worked very well with most of the 32 children; the resultant tape-recordings showed fascinating variation in terms of language ability and reasoning power; but on the page it looked and sounded very dominating, even domineering: all those questions and commands! My mainstream colleagues all gave it the thumbs down. It was not the sort of experience to encourage speaking and listening: too much teacher-talk.

The oral assessment exercise had come out of the experience of paired reading and collaborative story-making. It seemed to me, if not to anyone else, to be a very successful instrument with children who had been learning English for a term or more, but the absolute beginners needed a more trimmed down 'frame' to talk in; they needed more of what Bruner (1975) has termed 'scaffolding', while their command of the second language was under construction, as recommended in *Teaching Talking and Listening* (National Oracy Project, 1990: 20).

Perhaps I could find a way of letting *them* experience being the questioner. The result was the Language Master course which, when I was using it with children, I called 'What's this?' after the opening phrase. Since then, I have reflected that this is a very teacher-like question, and have changed the opening dialogue to 'What's that? It's a cat.' Other ESL tutors in Kent also used it and found it helpful, so it might have a wider usefulness still. I have given it an acronym: SLLIPs (Second Language Learners in Primary Schools). The course itself I renamed 'Eavesdroppers', for two reasons. There is a proverb: 'Eavesdroppers never hear good of themselves', and the children whom I taught to understand English were then able to hear pretty unflattering things said about them by some English people. Less politically, I felt that effectively overhearing conversational exchanges recorded on the machine *and taking part in them*, helped to provide the 'comprehensible input', which Krashen stresses the importance of, in second language acquisition.

The course consists of 50 short dialogue sequences, mainly brief question-and-answer exchanges visualised as taking place between two (native) speakers. These are intended to encourage from the outset the adoption by the learner of the intonation patterns, ellipses and elisions of natural speech in Standard English. A pre-recorded model produced by a native speaker should be ready on the upper band of the tape so that learners have the immediate option, even if working in isolation, of testing their pronunciation, intonation, listening comprehension, and near-native speed of delivery against native speech. The most productive use has been found to be as a paired activity between two learners, varying the roles of questioner and respondent by negotiation with each other and the teacher, whose presence and level of intervention should be increasingly noticeable by its absence. The teacher will have provided the model beforehand, out of the 'heat of the kitchen', when pre-recording the upper band of tape on each card. Intervention when the course is in use by the learner opens up the possibility, even likelihood, of the accidental and unintended introduction of typical patterns of contrastive stress ('teacher-talk'). These are easy to learn but hard to unlearn, when they have been acquired initially in an emotionally-fraught situation.

'Eavesdroppers' may by now sound very complicated and forbidding as an instrument for learning to speak and read Standard English; but it is not so in use. Adult and child speakers of first languages other than English have appeared to find it less intimidating than a judgmental human being who seemingly never makes mistakes and therefore finds making allowances for 'slips of the tongue' as difficult as would a science-fiction android! Unexpectedly, 'Eavesdroppers' has also proved useful for junior age children struggling to learn to speak, read and write Standard English in the classroom, when it is not the language which they use at home. The National Curriculum's definition of them is 'non-standard speakers'. Collectively they form a majority of native users of English at this stage of childhood; but since the English which they use is not adult Standard English, they are, apparently, to be taught that it is not acceptable and must be replaced. The consequences of such a policy remain to be seen.

References

Ashworth, E. (1988) *Language Policy in the Primary School: Content and Management.* Beckenham: Croom Helm.

Bruner, J.S. (1975) The ontogenesis of speech acts. *Journal of Child Language* 2, 1–20.

Dulay, H.C and Burt, M.K. (1974) You can't learn without goofing: An analysis of children's second-language errors. In J.C. Richards (ed.) *Error Analysis: Perspectives on Second Language Acquisition.* London: Longman.

Milroy, L. (1987) *Observing and Analysing Natural Language.* Oxford: Basil Blackwell.

National Oracy Project (1990) *Teaching Talking and Learning.* York: National Curriculum Council.

Tough, J. (1977) *Talking and Learning.* London: Ward Lock Educational and Drake Educational Associates.

Trudgill, P. (1975) *Accent, Dialect and the School.* London: Edward Arnold.

Wilkinson, A. (1963) *The Foundations of Language.* Oxford: Oxford University Press.

12 The Bilingual Child – Learning and Teaching in Multicultural Contexts: Summary of the Open Forum for Participants' Contributions

MAHENDRA K. VERMA and SALLY FIRTH

This plenary session was organised to provide an opportunity for the course participants to discuss issues which were of importance to them. The aim of the session was to allow further discussion of any of the issues which had been raised during the four days of the course, as well as to introduce any matters which had not been addressed at all. The participants were invited to put forward their own concerns, opinions and experiences. The session is presented here as an edited transcript. This format was chosen to ensure accurate representation of the contributors' views. It is followed by a summary of the discussion.

Key

A = Chair **B** = Support Teacher **C** = Support Teacher **D** = Support Teacher (in Wales) **E** = Head of Support Service **F** = Bilingual Support Teacher **G** = Bilingual Support Teacher **H** = Support Teacher **I** = Bilingual Support Teacher **J** = Support Teacher **K** = Support Teacher (in Wales) **L** = Bilingual Support Teacher **M** = Support Teacher (in Wales) **N** = Support Teacher **O** = Support Teacher **P** = Postgraduate Researcher and ESL Teacher **Q** = Qualified Teacher Status **R** = Support Teacher (in Wales) **S** = Support Teacher **T** = Bilingual Support Teacher **U** = Bilingual Support Teacher

A: How is the mother tongue harnessed in the classroom in your authority? [To B] Is there partnership between the support teacher and the class teacher? We have watched a video taken in your authority where both the support teacher and the class teacher were in class, and while the class teacher was introducing an activity, the support teacher was putting things on the wall or helping and generally supporting. Is that how it is still going on?

B: There is a huge range of different practices. There can be a huge gap between theory and practice. There are bilingual classroom assistants who work in that way, in a partnership where they are involved in the planning. You have got to be involved in the planning – you can't do it any other way and be effective. There is the constraint of time, but *some* schools are managing it. But it is not an ESL teacher's or a bilingual support teacher's responsibility; it's a management responsibility. It has to be managed. We must get in at the management level of schools first, so that there is an agreed approach.

C: Where I work, some schools are not used to having ethnic minority children and have never had Section 11 teachers in school before. Home Office money would be more wisely spent if somebody came in at the initial stages and talked to the teachers during INSETs about how Section 11 teachers are to be used and what to expect. This should come from the management level rather than being left to the Section 11 teacher on arrival.

B: It's your responsibility though.

C: No I don't think it is.

D: But in our school it *did* start with management and I *still* had the same problem.

C: I think a whole school INSET would be much easier though.

D: We didn't have INSETs, but we had input into staff meetings.

C: We were given nothing, and it had a really big knock-on effect on my relationship with the children, because until about half-term the children were convinced I was just a helper. They didn't realise what my role was at all.

A: Let's have some other comments from your experiences.

E: In my support service, we do not have bilingual assistants – it's up to the schools to provide their own.

A: Right, and have they appointed bilingual assistants?

E: They had a fair number before this new way of applying for Section 11 funding. Some of them have put in for Section 11 bilingual assistants; some of them have put in for Section 11 nursery nurses – depending upon money and how they see their needs. But I have very little to do with the assistants; they are controlled by the schools.

F: I think training is needed for awareness of the teachers – including

Section 11 teachers – because so many teachers just don't know how to deal with the needs of *all* the children. If you are in a situation where you are on your own, you need a network of support structure developing. In our authority, bilingual assistants have two weeks of intensive training at the beginning of the year. Then they are placed in the schools, but there are always Section 11 teachers who can support them in their role – delivering INSETs to *all* the staff to make sure that they understand the role of the bilingual assistant. If a bilingual assistant has a problem, he or she can always go to their team leader – they have got the support structure there for them. The training is to ensure that mainstream staff understand your role and that you understand their role.

A: Let's address the issue of preparing support assistants/teachers and class teachers to meet the challenges of the education of the bilingual child. Is there ongoing training for the teachers of bilingual children?

[Many of the participants shake their heads and say 'no', but a few say 'yes'.]

G: Our authority has recently reorganised its Section 11 teaching, and in fact we have a dual training programme which we partake in once every week, on Tuesday afternoon. One Tuesday every fortnight, we have the whole team back at the centre for the whole afternoon. Firstly we deal with the business matters, but that is only a short aspect. We designate the rest of the time (an hour and a half) to professional development. This involves everybody, including the instructors and bilingual classroom assistants.

And then every other Tuesday, we only have the bilingual classroom assistants present. We felt that they were crucial people and yet they did not come into teaching, or they *may* not come into teaching, with the teacher training that they would require – and yet, because they were expected to work alongside the teachers, at the same time they had a very specialist job. It is therefore important for them to know the elements of the teacher's training. So we have designed our own teaching programme where within a term's time, a language support teacher and a bilingual assistant working in the same school – maybe at the same time, maybe at different times, maybe with different teachers – begin to realise where they need to develop each other. And therefore every alternate Tuesday we come and share our good practice, and we are actually training each other. It is an ongoing programme. Bilingual classroom assistants had a very structured 10 week programme. But it hasn't finished; it is continuing – if someone says: 'Right, this is another problem that we have been faced with', the issues are discussed. It is therefore a building programme as well as a supporting programme.

A: That sounds very good.

F: I have an important point regarding training: how many mainstream teachers have come here? *Those* are the people we should be talking to. I always come to these courses because it's part of my role, but quite often, it's really mainstream staff who should be here. They're not here because their budgets are under pressure. So even though authorities run courses, mainstream teachers can't always attend because they would rather go on their SATs training. Schools are willing to pay £80 a day supply for two teachers to go on SATs training.

H: Our authority actually runs courses whereby each Section 11 teacher has to bring a mainstream teacher.

D: My situation is a bit different. On average there are only about three bilingual children in a class in the school. If there were more bilingual children, the teachers would maybe feel that they needed some strategies for coping. But in our school, it is the mainstream teachers who don't really see the need – and they *certainly* wouldn't agree with encouraging bilingualism. They see me as helping children to achieve skills in order to be able to accept the National Curriculum. Bilingualism would certainly never come into it – they're not interested.

A: We're not talking about bilingualism. We're talking about supporting bilingual children achieve what the National Curriculum and society and the community want them to achieve. And we're talking about the facilities to be offered to everyone who is contributing to this. What sort of facilities exist?

B: Like all schools, we have got five INSET days, and I think that is one forum where we can actually get support teachers and mainstream teachers together. That is a real place where we can target INSET, rather than forming our own Section 11 INSETs.

A: Does that happen in your authority?

B: We are trying to promote it – we've done a number since the reorganisation. It is a place where all the staff are present *plus* the management. If you organise it properly you can deal with those different levels.

A: Are there any more experiences from other counties?

I: In our county, we used to meet as a team on Thursdays for ongoing training, but since the new project has started we have just had five INSETs and five staff meetings. Apart from that we don't have any ongoing training. We are working in isolation – or talking to friends and colleagues about how we are doing. We haven't got any sort of training or INSETs with the mainstream.

A: How about you? [To J.]

J: Section 11 only came to us last year, so we were one of the last parts of the country to receive Section 11 funding. Because of that and because of the fund-cutting, they said: 'Right, you can have your teachers, you can have your language assistants, but forget any in-service training, forget any advisory service, forget any money. You've got three years – get on with it.' And that is what we are doing.

A: Get on with the job with no preparation at all?

J: Precisely.

K: You're not alone in that. We are exactly the same. We have no advisory service. We [referring to herself and her colleague beside her] are the advisory service. We have got to run a training day on Monday, with absolutely no notice, for the rest of our staff. We have no non-contact time – the co-ordinators have half a day non-contact time per week. But the rest of the staff have no non-contact time, so the only opportunities to get together are on training courses.

A: How about you? [To E.]

E: When I go round schools in my authority, I tell the headteachers that we provide INSETs under these headings. Sometimes they then ask for specific things. We had a nursery where a new headteacher had just started, and she felt that the bilingual assistant was being used dreadfully. It was a very awkward situation, because everybody had their little corners in the nursery. They had got walls and partitions, and they were all holding on to their own resources. They didn't want to share (I don't know why), and even after going in, it has made no difference whatsoever. We have sent somebody in from our team to try and break the ice a little. She has been going for six months, and she is still treated like somebody coming in to wash up the pots and make the coffee. She did it initially thinking: 'Well, if I do it now, then they'll all take their turns to do it, like a rota-system', but it never got to that. It was a case of: 'You don't have a class, therefore you're not a proper teacher'.

A: This is a very important statement: 'You don't have a class'. I have heard that so many times. Is that your experience? [To everybody.]

[Many nod and say 'yes'.]

F: It's the support structure that you need as well. For example, when we deal with a school we have got a whole-school policy, and if we run into problems then it is passed on to the heavies; it goes to the team leader and then to the section manager. You need that support structure to back up what you are trying to do, because you do come across situations where you can't deal with the management yourself.

Perhaps if it's at class teacher level, you can deal with it more easily. But if you are having to deal with the headteacher, you do need that support structure.

E: But in this case the headteacher is quite willing. It's not the headteacher who is the problem; it's the rest of the staff.

F: Yes, but the teacher who is working with that nursery nurse should know that she's not on her own, that she's got back-up.

A: What we have found when talking to support teachers is that the various job descriptions are there because they are the basis on which you apply for grants. But there are two things which we have heard. The job description is either not implementable because of all the things that are listed there, or that once the job is there and the money is received, then it is actually forgotten.

L: It is the attitude of the staff that must be changed. There is racism in the staffroom. Some of the staff I have come across didn't want the coloured children to be in the school, and say that they had no right to be in the school.

D: Yes, I have actually been told by a teacher that Section 11 funding is racist.

A: In what sense?

D: In that these children are being singled out and are having money pumped into their education. My argument is that the government pays the money and maybe they feel that it's now their turn to have a share in education. In my school it's very different because it's the whole teaching practice that I would scrap – not just for bilingual children, but all the way through.

M: In my experience, however badly things might have started off, a change of attitude towards the Section 11 teacher and the bilingual children comes once the class teacher starts to see a very definite improvement in the child's English, and therefore in the rest of the child's performance.

D: But I do have that from the teachers I work with – some of them come and say 'Look, look, isn't this marvellous?' But I still feel that they don't value the underlying *raison d'être*. In their eyes, it is all right as long as I can improve their reading skills and as long as they learn their sounds. There is one fourth year junior teacher who has four children in his class – the only four children in his class who are reading three or four years behind their chronological age – and he only hears them read once a week. And he's quite happy if I go in and do that. But I don't see that as my role – my role is basically to help those children and also to help him to change *his* practice in order to accommodate the children who are not achieving.

N: One of our problems came because we started off with Section 11 teaching our own pupils. And the teachers loved the idea of us going in, withdrawing a group of children and teaching them. They weren't interested in *what* we were teaching them, as long as we were teaching them and sending them back into the classroom at the end of the day. Now having gone in there to tell them those methods of teaching are out, they don't want to know – they are still trying to get them out. It's easier for them.

D: Yes, it makes their job easier. They want the tutoring. But our jobs ought to be alongside classroom teachers, helping them. They should see that it would make the National Curriculum easier for them if we all worked together.

H: I work exclusively in Science in secondary schools at the moment, and I've found that is the way in. I am a Science teacher and they know that, so in terms of equality I am just as good as them. And I've worked with Science but gradually brought in the other issues, so that what I do benefits bilingual pupils (that's what I'm there for) – but what I do also benefits *all* the pupils. In one school I've worked in for four years (working totally in the Science department), I've swung them round and there is now more partnership teaching and collaboration and group activity than there was originally. It's a very slow process and you have to go in where they are interested, and in secondary schools teachers are interested in their subject first and everything else second.

The Association of Science Education has published quite a few documents on multicultural issues and bilinguals in the classroom. In Science, the ASE set up a working party two and a half years ago which investigated this and published a number of documents which are quite good. Does anybody know of any other subject areas which have done this?

[There is no response from the floor.]

A: No. Can we move on to another question then? Do you ever get the chance to work with other children?

O: Yes, with the whole class. We also have a year plan for ourselves and for the bilingual classroom assistants to target areas of work.

A: What is your post?

O: Bilingual classroom teacher.

F: What other languages do you speak?

O: We are not bilingual; we support bilingual pupils.

P: I find this terminology very difficult.

A: It is – we have found this in our research.

O: Right at the beginning of this course we needed to clarify our understanding as it seemed to be different for different people.

A: I think that the authorities which have gone back to the old-fashioned title of 'ESL teachers' are perhaps more honest, because it seems to many of the teachers that they are asked to support *English* development, not bilingual development. So the point about supporting bilingualism, or 'bilingual support teachers' with a brief to support bilingualism, is not quite on the agenda.

F: 'Language support teacher' sounds so pathetic. It sounds like you're holding up their arm or their leg – whereas really you are propping the whole lot up: the classroom and the teacher. So I just don't like that title at all. It should become something like 'language specialist teacher' – and nothing including 'support'.

A: Moving on – does the school or LEA have a policy towards empowering the support staff by offering them facilities to gain QTS or offering them senior positions?

Several voices: What is QTS?

A: 'Qualified Teacher Status'. Quite a lot of support instructors or assistants feel that they are *not* empowered simply because the classroom teacher and other teachers who *have* got QTS think that they are not really qualified, and therefore that their role should be limited. If that is the case, is there a clear policy to empower them by offering them facilities to get QTS? There are various routes to QTS, which are often not known to these people because authorities do not want to tell these categories of people that it is possible to apply to get QTS. There are certain DES rules, but in the end it depends to a large extent on the recommendation of the headteacher and the adviser of the county for the DES to consider giving someone QTS.

The other point is that only if you get QTS can you become eligible to apply for senior positions. And there are some people with teaching qualifications and yet who are not in senior positions. This issue was discussed by various people in the authority where we have been working, because they are worried about what is going to happen after Section 11 money dries up (which it is going to do very soon) to these teachers who are there at the time when the mainstream teachers and the county needs them most. Is there a future plan in place in any of your authorities?

[There is no response from the floor.]

Has anyone got any example of good practice as far as empowering these support staff is concerned?

F: What is going to happen to us? – we're trained.

A: One possibility could be for your authority to be thinking in terms of offering you training opportunities so that after the end of Section 11 you could apply for other jobs – rather than being left out in the cold.

F: Schools are under tight budgets, aren't they?

H: Under LMS and GMS most authorities have very little power now.

A: Under LMS I am told that the governors and the headteachers have power. Are they doing anything?

H: Yes – laying off staff.

D: Theoretically speaking they have the opportunity to use the money how they see fit.

E: I know what a lot of schools will do – one school I know of got rid of five mainstream teachers last June and July on early retirement because they were too expensive, and they took on five probationists. If they get rid of another five this year for another five probationists, in a couple of years they are going to have inexperienced teachers running the school.

A: I know that you are all very motivated and committed – that's why you are there – but does it demotivate you to think that after two or three years there may be no route for you? Does it demotivate you to think that you are doing a good job, and yet that the authority and the schools and the headteachers might not take that into consideration?

F: I don't feel demotivated, but I feel young enough to move again and do something else.

D: At the end of the day, the best thing that could happen would be for us to go into mainstream classroom teaching, to bring proper practice into what's happening in the mainstream.

We have been told by the centre that when schools go on to LMS, there is this possibility for schools to spend their money how they want.

H: It's all market forces and money. One school I've worked in has been running at an £80,000 deficit for the last five years. Most of the teachers have been there a long time and what they'll do now they have gone GMS is start to get rid of those teachers. The bottom line is money. Educationally speaking, it is brilliant to have two adults in the classroom – or three even – as this school actually has done over the last three years, but now that money is the bottom line, that will go out of the window.

Q: [To A] At the end of your study, are you going to sit on the fence, like most other people do?

A: I've never been on the fence.

Q: In that case, I will be very pleased because too many people are frightened of saying things. How much have we achieved through this form of agenda (and I'm not saying that it shouldn't exist)? Very little. We have only been talking to the converted so far. As you said a few moments ago, the governing bodies are the people who will be in a position to hire or fire people – and therefore people like us should be talking to them. I have been a governor in three schools, I am also a QTS teacher, and I am in a borough without a plan for QTS teachers – the way things are going is absolutely diabolical on every front. So what I think one has to do is go back to the community, go back to the people, back the *right* governors, and tell them to pose questions to the management such as: 'What are you going to do about the plight of these people who are persistently underachieving?' Teachers in the mainstream, senior teachers, advisers, and directors of the LEA have condoned the failure of these children.

A: Are you aware of parents of bilingual children who are governors of the schools in which you work?

[Many participants shake their heads and say no.]

H: There are a few but they are in a minority.

D: One has been elected in our school, but in actual fact during the whole of the time she sat on the board, she never contributed anything. It was very sad, because the thing was that she was the wrong person. She is a very quiet person, she's not forceful enough, and she was probably extremely intimidated by it all.

A: Are any of these governors invited to your INSETs? Has a bilingual parent who is a governor of the school *ever* been invited?

['Never' is the reply.]

A: Never. That would be one of the ways in which you could highlight your...

C: The teachers would say no.

F: Yes, and it can also mean taking time off work. All the governors from our school were openly invited to all the INSETs, but they had jobs and businesses.

A: But perhaps the Heads of Service could work harder to attract those parent governors who are bilingual, because after all, in future if it's going to be effective, parent power or governor power is going to govern the curriculum or the pace at which things are implemented in schools. If that is going to be effective, these bilingual governors should not only be interested in the budget of the school, they should actually be interested in specific issues, especially the bilingual children's issues. And one way in which it can be done is by inviting them to INSETs where they could meet each individual, whether it is a nursery nurse, a bilingual assistant or instructor, or a bilingual classroom teacher so that they could share the issues and anxieties with them.

H: But bilingual governors are in a minority. In all the schools that I work in, if there *is* an ethnic minority governor, they are in the minority – and basically, what the rest want is totally different. A number of schools where I work will change the goalposts of entry, now they've gone GMS. They will reduce their ethnic minority intake, because they are bottom of the league tables. They will say: 'Bilingual pupils underachieve, therefore we don't want them.'

C: I think we should be educating all governors. Part of the reason why I'm so scared of them is because they're not very well informed. The head of our governing body actually believes that we all ought to have our salaries frozen so that the school can afford to buy more resources. And they've got a lot of power, so we do need to enlighten *all* governors.

A: So don't the governor training programmes take into account any of these issues, because I am told that governors have training and tax-payers' money is spent on that. Perhaps they are not well informed simply because these issues are not important to them.

Q: There is another underlying current going on at the moment. The LEAs want as many secondary schools to stay with them as possible, and in order for those schools to stay with them, what most of the LEAs are trying to do is to hand-pick the governors. They are choosing governors who can influence schools to stay with the LEA. I will certainly be voicing my opinion and saying that this is not on, and we will definitely try and explore the other path. Although I'm not personally in favour of the opting-out system, I will not hesitate in doing this in order to put those people in their places.

There is another trend, which concerns community governors: they always choose the people who allow themselves to be patronised by the heads and by the LEA advisers and inspectors. When I was the governor of three schools, I stood up to them, I walked out, I put them on the grill many times, and today I'm no good. Why? Because they consider me to be a trouble-maker. And this is where you come in as teachers. There are so many good governors amongst the ethnic minorities – go to the good ones, and say: 'Come on, join us, we need you'. And I can assure you they will all listen to you.

P: On a positive note, if it is possible for parents' desires for their children's bilingualism to be respected, if the parents' power can be mobilised, the recognition of bilingualism as a positive factor in children's learning can be established much more by parents and by community action than by anything else – as demonstrated in Wales.

A: Let's turn our attention to the use of the mother tongue. To what extent do you use the mother tongue or allow the child to use their mother tongue for meaningful communication in the classroom? And to what extent do the monolingual teachers accept the use of the mother tongue as pedagogically sound?

R: I am a monolingual teacher with no bilingualism, but I encourage it.

A: How about the classroom teacher?

R: Oh yes, they love it. I think we're actually quite lucky in our authority in Wales.

A: Since P mentioned Wales and we have colleagues from Wales, can I ask you as teachers, whether you are doing anything at all to encourage the authority to move on to a model which they have for the Welsh children in terms of bilingualism?

R: Well we do have quite a problem here. I actually use Welsh as well as English. I have to speak Welsh first and English next, because we teach in both languages.

We have no money for the service we have. We actually run the service ourselves with no finances. We are very envious of the Welsh as a Second Language Service because they have got an enormous amount of money.

A: But perhaps you would have an enormous amount of money too if you put forward the argument that the Panjabi child, like the Welsh speaking child, should also be in the same curriculum – in the sense that there should be status accorded to Panjabi: Panjabi as a language, Panjabi as a medium of instruction. Do you feel committed enough to tell the authority: 'Since we have got this programme for the Welsh mother tongue speakers, why can't we have the same programme, which is cognitively and pedagogically sound, for the Urdu and the Panjabi and the Chinese children?'

K: We feel committed enough.

A: But do you actually propose this, do you argue for this?

K: Well it's getting somebody to argue with that's the problem.

A: You have contact with the authorities, you interact with other people in the authority, don't you?

D: I do on a personal level in school because I'm committed to that. But as far as promoting it with the authority is concerned, I don't think I ever really see anybody from the authority.

A: What do you think the Welsh LEAs' general policy is going to be in the next few years as far as the black bilingual children and their mother tongues are concerned?

B: Well the authorities are being swept away and they're going to be brought down to practically parish level.

D: That's right, they're restructuring.

P: They are being abolished so even if the teacher *did* liaise with them successfully, they've only got another two years anyway and then they're going.

A: Yes, but while they are there, they can put forward the argument on the agenda.

S: One problem in authorities like these, where the ethnic minority populations are very sparsely spread, is that you don't have the political pull. They say you're not politically relevant. So although they might be sympathetic, they're not going to put the money there.

C: Even if it is economically viable and it should have been in the area where I used to work, even where you can do mother tongue work in a really meaningful way and where children use their mother tongue as an extra-curricular resource, mother tongue support is *still* not provided. I had no mother tongue support because I was in a junior class and my headteacher said: 'You don't need it; the children's English is already good enough'. So really all it is being used for is to develop English until children are competent – and that's not the way that we have been talking about using the mother tongue.

A: So you are saying that it is not only the supporters who are used as a crutch, but that the children's mother tongue is also used as a crutch in order to achieve competency in English.

D: What about parental attitudes? – I had to really struggle to say to parents 'Please – your mother tongue is important.'

C: That is why they've got that attitude, and I'm sure that is why the children have that attitude – the children I worked with in that school didn't have any respect for their mother tongue. They were *really* embarrassed by it.

[Several other participants agree.]

K: In our situation there is a great gap, in that bilingualism in English and Welsh or a European language or Japanese is valued and seen as a positive thing, but that being bilingual in English and an ethnic minority community language is still not valued.

[Several others agree.]

H: A lot of schools in my authority used to teach Urdu when Section 11 allowed it, but as soon as the Section 11 funding was taken away, that was it.

E: The Inspectors in our authority say that because community languages are there in the National Curriculum, they *are* given the same status as the European languages, and therefore it is up to the secondary schools to provide the teaching out of their own budgets, and it is up to the parents to put pressure on.

D: Yes, at the end of the day, the parents have a great responsibility. In real terms they have the power because they vote.

E: They come to me, and they say 'What can you do?'. I can't do anything. I say 'I will tell you what to do, I will write letters for you, to your school. Because all it needs is 50 of you to go to a PTA meeting to swing the vote your way.' I mean you can't get 50 English people turning up.

Q: In 1988, my local borough invited me to sit on their working party to look into the provision of community languages. The first thing we did was that we were able to get a £250,000 budget. We had a well-defined job description of the Community Languages Co-ordinator. And they deliberately employed the person who was a senile male waiting to retire and loved to sit in his chair in the teachers' centre – despite the fact that on the job description it was very clearly written that he would have to spend $X\%$ of his time going to the people, going to the parents, going to the headteachers and discussing the policy matters, and reporting back to the people who are in turn responsible, in terms of line management. First the budget started getting reduced, and now they have put the whole system on a life-support. That is, they go to a few councillors and say: 'Would you vote for me? I've got £50,000 for Panjabi teaching.' The answer is 'Yeah, yeah, no problem', but none of those people ever say 'What has been achieved so far? You're paying for these people, there is one person on £30–40,000 sitting there, there is another Co-ordinator doing exactly the same, and neither of them go and liaise with the people.' Why are they doing it? Because the authority knows that when the time comes, they can switch it off under the excuse that they provided three people at so much money, and nothing was achieved. They have encouraged the whole thing to fail, and us lot, and the parents, the governors, the community leaders and the councillors, never bothered to put them on the spot saying: 'Why is there no performance level for those people, why is there no accountability?' Why don't we do it? Because it suits the system to have a policy like this – and that is where the problem is.

E: Well, I think that we have to stand up and say there are Asian teachers who are not doing their job. I don't think that people should shy back from that.

Q: Absolutely.

E: I had an awful problem with one of my staff, and in the end I made life so difficult for her that she had to leave. I said: 'Either you do your job or you get out'.

Q: Regarding the status of people like us, we either have to speak out, or get shut out, despite a parity in terms of linguistic and intellectual levels. And inside a classroom situation what is the status of the language assistants or the people who are teaching with QTS? If the children identify themselves with those people and say 'He/she is from my culture', what have they achieved?

Not giving us status and recognition suits the system. Unless the group gets together, organises and mobilises themselves, and puts political pressure on those at the top, nothing will happen.

T: We have a very active racial equality council with whom we work very closely. It is through the racial equality council that we got our Section 11 funding, that we got Urdu on offer in our secondary schools, and that we have governor representatives.

A: Since we have been talking about parents, what role do parents play in the process of assessment of their children?

[Several participants answer 'none'.]

Q: They go to people like E, and they say: 'My child's future is in your hands. Please do whatever you can.' That is the attitude of our parents.

A: Does assessment take place in the context of the classroom and the curriculum by as many staff, including the bilingual support assistants and teachers, as possible?

H: Last year in one of the schools I worked in, when they did the SATs, they had approximately 15 teachers, bilingual assistants, people who were with children doing SATs.

A: Are you talking about a secondary school?

H: Yes. And it's all money dependent.

A: How about your experience? [To T]

T: They just used me for some of the Science experiments, but otherwise they said they could do it themselves.

L: I worked with the Chinese children – but I wasn't given any extra money or extra pay. That was my own time.

A: What about you? [To U]

U: No, I wasn't used.

A: As a Head of Service, are you conscious of this? [To E] Your bilingual staff are used as an aid, they teach, they contribute, but when the *crucial* time of assessment comes, which is going to contribute to league tables, what is there that you, as a Head of Service, can do to convince the class teachers and the headteachers that they should use the bilingual support staff?

E: The problem is that there are only five of us who are bilingual in the service, so it's just not feasible anyway. You can do it for some, but you can't do it for others. And it is really unfair, especially as league tables are going to be published, but there is nothing we can do when there are not enough staff. For example, I have only one Bengali teacher to cover the whole authority.

A: Does it mean that there are schools where there are bilingual children, whether they are isolated or whether there are several, which do not have either a resident bilingual support or a peripatetic teacher?

[Most of those present say 'yes'.]

A: So in your authorities are there schools where there is no support available at all?

E: Yes, we have to turn schools down.

D: Do you mean bilingual support? [To A]

A: By bilingual support I don't mean supporting the mother tongue, because that is not something which is allowed within the National Curriculum so to say – although individual authorities have their own policies. So are there schools with potentially bilingual children with no support?

[Several participants answer 'yes'.]

E: After the Home Office money runs out, in our LEA we will try to get as much money as we can to run the support service. And when there are 10 staff, you need an awful lot of money to run it. Then the LEA had the fantastic idea that after the project money runs out, they would sell us to schools. Now if you've got two children in your school, and they need help – and the authority thought they would charge about £50 a day for us to go into a school – I don't think that any school would be willing to pay £50 a day for two pupils in their school. They would say: 'We'll make do with what we have'.

A: It's market forces again. Let's consider one more question: to what extent does *bias* covertly or overtly influence the assessment? Have you felt that bias, in various forms, has actually penetrated or influenced assessment?

F: It's not just the bilingual children – bias affects them all.

A: What sort of bias do you think may have affected the assessment of children who are not bilingual?

F: I remember one Science SAT where the children had to look at different types of light, like direct light from a lamp, and light cast on a ceiling. But it was really useless because it was on a picture, and how can you see light on a picture? There were lots of things like that that children were just not familiar with. There was one about an echo in a cave this year. Children might not have always been to a cave, and you can't bring a cave in, into the classroom. And there is a picture of a person standing there showing their voice in waves. Furthermore, children have to give a certain worded response. For example, there was one on shadow and they had to say that the light *was passed through* ... And if they said anything other than that, they were wrong. They may well have understood the concept and shown you where the shadow was, but worded it differently, so they were marked as not reaching that level.

A: These are things that you say are applicable to all pupils; are there any specific examples where you think that something was marked wrong simply because the assessor was not aware of the experiences that the black child had?

H: Yes, in Key Stage 3 last year there was a question on a springboard in a swimming pool, and how many Muslim girls go swimming? I must say though that my personal experience was that when the teachers were marking, there was a bias towards the pupils. The school that I worked in last year actually bent the rules greatly.

F: It's because teachers know their pupils.

A: Is there anything else you want to raise? Are there any other things you wish to talk about?

F: I just feel like I'm chipping away at this huge brick wall and somebody on top is making it bigger and bigger and bigger.

Summary

The first topic raised concerned *preparing support assistants/teachers and class teachers to meet the challenges of the education of the bilingual child.* The questions discussed were:

(1)   Are class teachers encouraged to work with support assistants/ teachers as equal partners?

(2)   Is there on-going training for the teachers of bilingual children?

(3)   Does the school/LEA have a policy towards empowering the support staff by:
      (a) offering them facilities to gain Qualified Teacher Status;
      (b) offering them senior positions?

The response to question 1 was that it varies between individuals. The view was expressed that responsibility should be taken on at the management level of schools in order to improve the situation. Another participant suggested that prior to a Section 11 teacher starting to work in a school, an INSET should be held for the whole school in order to explain the role of that support teacher. The need for a network of support structure to back up the support teacher or assistant when there are problems was also highlighted.

In response to question 2, many of those present answered that there was no ongoing training for the teachers of bilingual children. A representative from one authority told the floor that they had been given a sum of Section 11 money sufficient to employ some language assistants, but that they were allowed no preparation or in-service training whatsoever. One participant did answer positively, though, and gave details of the training programme in her authority. One support teacher pointed out that it is the mainstream staff who need to attend such training courses, but that their priorities were always with different areas of training such as courses concerning SATs.

A few of the participants called for a change in the attitude of mainstream staff, as some class teachers believe Section 11 funding to be racist because 'these children are being singled out and are having money pumped into their education'. Another participant informed the floor that racism still exists in the staffroom, to the extent that some teachers had been heard to say that ethnic minority children had no right to be in the school. Another support teacher pointed out that teachers used to be quite happy, though, when the method of teaching was to withdraw a group of children from their classroom for the whole day.

The various job titles of support teachers were then briefly discussed. While there has been a change in many authorities from the title of 'ESL Teacher' to 'Bilingual Support/Classroom Teacher', it was explained that this title is still problematic. That is, although they support bilingual children, many of these teachers are monolingual English speakers and therefore cannot support and develop the children's bilingualism as such.

There was no response to question 3, as discussion of a separate issue was embarked upon. This concerned *what the future holds for both bilingual children and support teachers after Section 11 funding ceases.* One participant claimed that the best outcome would be if support teachers could go into mainstream teaching, thereby bringing better practice into the classroom. As schools have to manage their own budgets under LMS, it was predicted that they would not spend money on having more than one teacher in the classroom. Furthermore, it was surmised that GMS schools will reduce their intake of ethnic minority children, supposedly to improve their chances of climbing up the league tables.

It was pointed out that in schools under GMS the power will be with the parents and governors. As the course participants knew of very few ethnic minority governors, it was claimed that little will therefore be implemented in favour of the bilingual pupils. Furthermore, one participant claimed that the few ethnic minority governors that did exist were often chosen because they had a quiet and submissive personality. According to some of those present, there should, therefore, not only be an attempt to increase the number of ethnic minority governors, but there must also be an effort to make *all* governors aware of the importance of the needs of bilingual children.

The next topic raised concerned the *use of the mother tongue*. The questions posed were:

(4) To what extent do you use the mother tongue or allow the child to use their mother tongue for meaningful communication?
(5) To what extent do the monolingual teachers accept the use of the mother tongue as pedagogically sound?

One of the support teachers working in a Welsh authority answered that both she and the class teachers encouraged use of the mother tongue despite being monolingual themselves. The participants working in Wales were then asked whether they were campaigning for the same bilingual programme for children who speak a community language such as Panjabi or Chinese as exists for children whose mother tongue is Welsh. It was claimed that authorities would probably not fund such a programme where the ethnic minority populations are quite sparsely spread. However, another support teacher pointed out that in her experience even authorities with a vast number of children sharing the same language, where mother tongue support *would* be economically viable, will not provide such support. The underlying reason seems to be that for authorities the goal for such children is competency *in English*. The value of bilingualism is still not recognised, unless it is bilingualism in English and Welsh or a European language or Japanese, for example.

The final topic raised concerned *current assessment practices*. The questions discussed were:

(6) What role do parents play in the process of assessment of their children?
(7) Does assessment take place in the context of the classroom and the curriculum by as many staff as possible – including bilingual support assistants and teachers?
(8) To what extent does *bias* overtly or covertly influence assessment?

In response to question 6, several participants answered that parents played no role. The response to question 7 was that many support teachers were not used during SATs assessment. One bilingual participant *was* used, but had to work in her own time with no extra pay. Regarding bilingual staff, one Head of Service pointed out that in her authority there were not enough such teachers in the service, meaning that many schools which requested bilingual support during SATs received none. Many more participants informed the chair that there are schools with potentially bilingual children in their authorities who receive no support. The Head of Service revealed that after Home Office funding expires her LEA was considering selling support teachers to schools – at a rate of about £50 per day. She pointed out that this plan would be detrimental to the education of bilingual children, because schools with fewer pupils in need of support would not be prepared to pay this.

In response to question 8, several examples were given of tasks which contained bias towards all pupils, and one was given which contained specific bias towards Muslim girls. On a positive note, though, one participant did point out that in his experience, teachers were biased in favour of the pupils when marking.

Finally, as the odds are stacked against support teachers (with the end of Section 11 funding and the switch to LMS and GMS for many schools), the negative comment offered by a bilingual support teacher at the close of the session was hardly surprising: 'I just feel like I'm chipping away at this huge brick wall and somebody on top is making it bigger and bigger and bigger'. But possible ways of combatting future problems *had* been suggested and shared in this plenary session, and hopefully, at the end of the course, the participants would have left feeling less isolated in their chipping!

Index

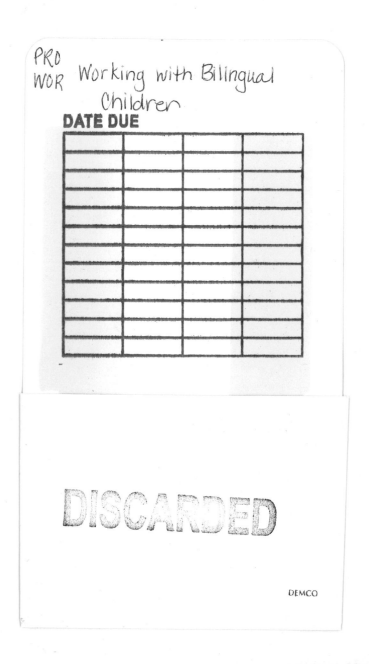

PRO
WOR Working with Bilingual
Children

DATE DUE

DISCARDED

DEMCO

Printed in the United States
25529LVS00001B/253-267

9 781853 592935